Service Offerings and Agreements
ITIL® Intermediate Capability Handbook

***it*SMF International**
The IT Service Management Forum

London: TSO

information & publishing solutions

Published by TSO (The Stationery Office)
and available from:

Online
www.tsoshop.co.uk

Mail, Telephone, Fax & E-mail
TSO
PO Box 29, Norwich, NR3 1GN
Telephone orders/General enquiries:
0870 600 5522
Fax orders: 0870 600 5533
E-mail: customer.services@tso.co.uk
Textphone: 0870 240 3701

TSO@Blackwell and other Accredited Agents

The AXELOS logo is a trade mark of
AXELOS Limited

The AXELOS swirl logo is a trade mark of
AXELOS Limited

ITIL® is a registered trade mark of
AXELOS Limited

MSP® is a registered trade mark of
AXELOS Limited

P3O® is a registered trade mark of
AXELOS Limited

PRINCE2® is a registered trade mark of
AXELOS Limited

M_o_R® is a registered trade mark of
AXELOS Limited

The Best Management Practice Official Publisher
logo is a trade mark of AXELOS Limited

A CIP catalogue record for this book is available
from the British Library

A Library of Congress CIP catalogue record has
been applied for

First edition 2010
Second edition 2014
First published 2014

ISBN 9780113314492 Single copy ISBN
ISBN 9780113314508 (Sold in a pack of 10 copies)

Printed in the United Kingdom for The
Stationery Office

Material is FSC certified. Sourced from
responsible sources

P002647005   11/14

Contents

Acknowledgements

SECOND EDITION

Author

Tricia Lewin, independent consultant, UK

Reviewers

Stuart Rance, Optimal Service Management

Marcus Vickery, QICT Limited

Paul Wigzel, Paul Wigzel Training & Consultancy

Series editor

Alison Cartlidge, Steria

FIRST EDITION

Authors

Alison Cartlidge, Steria

Janaki Chakravarthy, independent consultant, UK

Additional content: Ashley Hanna, HP, UK

Reviewers

Luci Allen, Pink Elephant, UK

Aidan Lawes, service management evangelist, UK

Tricia Lewin, independent consultant, UK

Trevor Murray, The Grey Matters, UK

Michael Imhoff Nielsen, IBM, Denmark

Sue Shaw, Tricentrica, UK

HP Suen, The Hong Kong Jockey Club

Editors

Alison Cartlidge, Steria

Mark Lillycrop, *it*SMF UK

About this guide

This guide provides a quick reference to the processes covered by the ITIL® service offerings and agreements (SOA) syllabus. It is designed to act as a study aid for students taking the ITIL Capability qualification for SOA, and as a handy portable reference source for practitioners who work with these processes.

This guide is not intended to replace the more detailed ITIL publications (Cabinet Office, 2011), nor to be a substitute for a course provider's training materials. Many parts of the syllabus require candidates to achieve competence at Bloom Levels 3 and 4, showing the ability to apply their learning and analyse a situation. This study aid focuses on the core knowledge that candidates need to acquire at Bloom Levels 1 and 2, including a knowledge and comprehension of the material that supports the syllabus.

Further information on the ITIL qualification scheme, including the ITIL glossary, can be found at:

www.axelos.com

Listed below in alphabetical order are the ITIL service management processes with cross-references to the publication in which they are primarily defined, and where significant further expansion is provided. Most processes play a role during each lifecycle stage, but only significant references are included. Those processes and functions specifically relevant to the SOA syllabus and covered in this guide are ticked.

ITIL service management processes

Service management process	SOA syllabus	Primary source	Further expansion
Access management		SO	
Availability management		SD	CSI
Business relationship management	✔	SS	SD, CSI
Capacity management		SD	SO, CSI
Change evaluation		ST	
Change management		ST	
Demand management	✔	SS	SD
Design coordination		SD	
Event management		SO	
Financial management for IT services	✔	SS	
Incident management		SO	CSI
Information security management		SD	SO
IT service continuity management		SD	
Knowledge management		ST	CSI
Problem management		SO	
Release and deployment management		ST	
Request fulfilment		SO	

Service management process	SOA syllabus	Primary source	Further expansion
Service asset and configuration management		ST	
Service catalogue management	✔	SD	SS
Service level management	✔	SD	SS, CSI
Service portfolio management	✔	SS	SD
Service validation and testing		ST	
Seven-step improvement process		CSI	
Strategy management for IT services		SS	
Supplier management	✔	SD	
Transition planning and support		ST	
Function			
Application management		SO	
IT operations management		SO	
Service desk		SO	
Technical management		SO	

SS *ITIL Service Strategy*; SD *ITIL Service Design*; ST *ITIL Service Transition*; SO *ITIL Service Operation*; CSI *ITIL Continual Service Improvement*

1 Introduction to service management

Note that cross-references in the headings are to section numbers in the ITIL core publications (Cabinet Office, 2011), where more detail can be found. The abbreviations used are: SS *ITIL Service Strategy*; SD *ITIL Service Design*; ST *ITIL Service Transition*; SO *ITIL Service Operation*; and CSI *ITIL Continual Service Improvement*. The core publications are listed in the 'Further guidance and contact points' section at the end.

1.1 BEST PRACTICE (SS 2.1.7)

Organizations operating in dynamic environments need to improve their performance and maintain competitive advantage. Adopting best practices in industry-wide use can help to improve capability.

Sources for best practice include:

- **Public frameworks and standards** These have been validated across diverse environments; knowledge is widely distributed among professionals; there is publicly available training and certification; acquisition of knowledge through the labour market is easier, as is collaboration and coordination across organizations
- **Proprietary knowledge of organizations and individuals** This is customized for the local context and specific business needs. It may only be available under commercial terms; it may also be tacit knowledge (i.e. inextricable and poorly documented).

Organizations should cultivate their own proprietary knowledge on top of a body of knowledge based on public frameworks and standards.

1.2   THE ITIL FRAMEWORK (SS 1.2, 1.4)

The ITIL framework is a source of best practice in service management. It is:

- Vendor-neutral
- Non-prescriptive
- Best practice.

ITIL is successful because it describes practices that enable organizations to deliver benefits, return on investment and sustained success. This means that organizations can:

- Deliver value for customers through services, improving customer relationships
- Integrate the strategy for services with the business strategy and customer needs
- Measure, monitor and optimize IT services and service provider performance, and reduce costs
- Manage the IT investment and budget, risks, knowledge, capabilities and resources to deliver services effectively and efficiently
- Enable adoption of a standard approach to service management across the enterprise
- Change the organizational culture to support the achievement of sustained success.

ITIL guidance can be found in the following sets of publications:

- **ITIL core** Best-practice publications applicable to all types of organizations that provide services to a business
- **ITIL complementary guidance** A set of publications with guidance specific to industry sectors, organization types, operating models and technology architectures.

ITIL guidance can be adapted to support various business environments and organizational strategies. Complementary ITIL publications provide flexibility to implement the core in a diverse range of environments.

ITIL has been deployed successfully around the world for more than 20 years. Over this time, the framework has evolved from a specialized set of service management topics with a focus on function, to a process-based framework, which now provides a broader holistic service lifecycle.

> **Definition: service lifecycle**
>
> An approach to IT service management that emphasizes the importance of coordination and control across the various functions, processes and systems necessary to manage the full lifecycle of IT services. The service lifecycle approach considers the strategy, design, transition, operation and continual improvement of IT services. Also known as service management lifecycle.

The service lifecycle is described in the five ITIL core publications. Each of these covers a stage of the service lifecycle (see Figure 1.1), from the initial definition and analysis of business requirements in *ITIL Service Strategy* and *ITIL Service Design,* through migration into the live environment within *ITIL Service Transition*, to live operation and improvement in *ITIL Service Operation* and *ITIL Continual Service Improvement.*

Figure 1.1 The service lifecycle

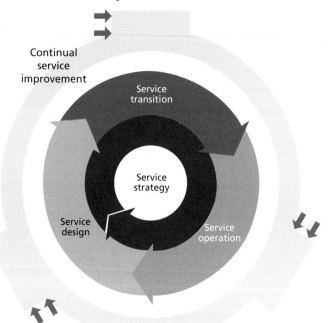

1.3   SERVICE MANAGEMENT (SS 2.1)

To understand what service management is, we need to
understand what services are, and how service management
can help service providers to deliver and manage these services.

Definition: service

A means of delivering value to customers by facilitating
outcomes customers want to achieve without the ownership
of specific costs and risks. The term 'service' is sometimes used
as a synonym for core service, IT service or service package.

Definition: IT service

A service provided by an IT service provider. An IT service is
made up of a combination of information technology, people
and processes. A customer-facing IT service directly supports
the business processes of one or more customers and its service
level targets should be defined in a service level agreement
(SLA). Other IT services, called supporting services, are not
directly used by the business but are required by the service
provider to deliver customer-facing services.

The outcomes that customers want to achieve are the reason
why they purchase or use a service. The value of the service to
the customer is directly dependent on how well a service
facilitates these outcomes.

Definition: outcome

The result of carrying out an activity, following a process, or
delivering an IT service etc. The term is used to refer to
intended results as well as to actual results.

Services facilitate outcomes by enhancing the performance of associated tasks and reducing the effect of constraints. These constraints may include regulation, lack of funding or capacity, or technology limitations. The end result is an increase in the probability of desired outcomes. While some services enhance performance of tasks, others have a more direct impact – performing the task itself. Services can be classified as:

- **Core services** These deliver the basic outcomes desired by one or more customers
- **Enabling services** These are needed in order for a core service to be delivered
- **Enhancing services** These are added to core services to make them more appealing to the customer.

Service management enables service providers to:

- Understand the services they are providing
- Ensure that the services really do facilitate the outcomes their customers want to achieve
- Understand the value of the services to their customers
- Understand and manage all of the costs and risks associated with those services.

Definition: service management

A set of specialized organizational capabilities for providing value to customers in the form of services.

These 'specialized organizational capabilities' are described in this guide. They include the processes, activities, functions and roles that service providers use to enable them to deliver services to their customers, as well as the ability to organize, manage knowledge, and understand how to facilitate outcomes that create value. However, service management is more than just a set of capabilities. It is also a professional practice supported by an extensive body of knowledge, experience and skills, with formal schemes for the education, training and certification of practising organizations.

Service management is concerned with more than just delivering services. Each service, process or infrastructure component has a lifecycle, and service management considers the entire lifecycle from strategy through design and transition to operation and continual improvement.

All IT organizations should act as service providers, using the principles of service management to ensure that they deliver the outcomes required by their customers.

> **Definition: IT service management (ITSM)**
>
> The implementation and management of quality IT services that meet the needs of the business. IT service management is performed by IT service providers through an appropriate mix of people, process and information technology.

1.4   PROCESSES AND FUNCTIONS (SS 2.2.2, 2.2.3)

> **Definition: process**
>
> A process is a structured set of activities designed to accomplish a specific objective. A process takes one or more defined inputs and turns them into defined outputs. It may include any of the roles, responsibilities, tools and management controls required to reliably deliver the outputs. A process may define policies, standards, guidelines, activities and work instructions if they are needed.

Processes define actions, dependencies and sequence. Processes have the following characteristics:

- **Measurability** Processes can be measured and performance-driven, in management terms such as cost and quality, and in practitioner terms such as duration and productivity
- **Specific results** Processes exist to deliver a specific result that is identifiable and countable
- **Customers** Processes deliver their primary results to customers or stakeholders, either internal or external, to meet their expectations
- **Responsiveness to specific triggers** Processes may be ongoing or iterative, but should be traceable to a specific trigger.

The key outputs from any process are driven by the objectives and include process measurement, reports and improvement. For the process to be effective, process outputs have to conform to operational norms derived from business objectives. For the process to be efficient, process activities have to be undertaken with the minimum resources. Figure 1.2 illustrates a process model.

Figure 1.2 Process model

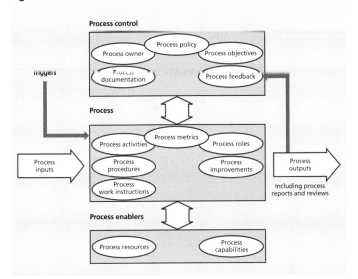

An organization needs to clearly define the roles and responsibilities required to undertake the processes and activities involved in each lifecycle stage. These roles are assigned to individuals within an organizational structure of teams, groups or functions.

Definition: function

A team or group of people and the tools or other resources they use to carry out one or more processes or activities – for example, the service desk.

Functions are self-contained, and have the capabilities and resources necessary for their performance and outcomes. They provide organizations with structure and stability. Coordination between functions through shared processes is a common organizational design.

ITIL Service Operation describes the service desk, technical management, IT operations management and application management functions in detail, with technical and application management providing the technical resources and expertise to manage across the whole service lifecycle.

1.5 ROLES

A role is a set of responsibilities, activities and authorities granted to a person or team. A role is defined in a process or function. One person or team may have multiple roles. ITIL does not describe all the roles that could possibly exist in an organization, but provides representative examples to aid in an organization's definition of its own roles.

Roles fall into two main categories – generic roles (e.g. process owner) and specific roles that are involved within a particular lifecycle stage or process. Generic roles are described below, while specific roles are covered in the relevant lifecycle chapters of the core ITIL publications.

Note that 'service manager' is a generic term for any manager within the service provider. The term is commonly used to refer to a business relationship manager, a process manager or a senior manager with responsibility for IT services overall. A service manager is often assigned several roles such as business relationship management, service level management and continual service improvement.

1.5.1   Process owner (SS 6.8.2)

The process owner role is accountable for ensuring that a process is fit for purpose, i.e. that it is capable of meeting its objectives; that it is performed according to the agreed and documented standard, and that it meets the aims of the process definition. This role may be assigned to the same person carrying out the process manager role.

Key accountabilities include:

■ Sponsoring, designing and change managing the process and its metrics
■ Defining the process strategy, with periodic reviews to keep current, and assisting with process design
■ Defining appropriate policies and standards for the process, with periodic auditing to ensure compliance
■ Communicating process information or changes as appropriate to ensure awareness
■ Providing process resources to support activities required throughout the service lifecycle
■ Ensuring that process technicians understand their role and have the required knowledge to deliver the process
■ Addressing issues with the running of the process
■ Identifying enhancement and improvement opportunities and making improvements to the process.

1.5.2   Process manager (SS 6.8.3)

The process manager role is accountable for operational management of a process. There may, for example, be several process managers for one process in different locations. This role may be assigned to the same person carrying out the process owner role.

Key accountabilities include:

- Working with the process owner to plan and coordinate all process activities
- Ensuring that all activities are carried out as required throughout the service lifecycle
- Appointing people to the required roles and managing assigned resources
- Working with service owners and other process managers to ensure the smooth running of services
- Monitoring and reporting on process performance
- Identifying opportunities for and making improvements to the process.

1.5.3   Process practitioner (SS 6.8.4)

A process practitioner is responsible for carrying out one or more process activities. This role may be assigned to the same person carrying out the process manager role.

Responsibilities typically include:

- Carrying out one or more activities of a process
- Understanding how his or her role contributes to the overall delivery of service and creation of value for the business
- Working with other stakeholders, such as line managers, co-workers, users and customers, to ensure that their contributions are effective
- Ensuring that the inputs, outputs and interfaces for his or her activities are correct
- Creating or updating records to show that activities have been carried out correctly.

1.5.4   Service owner (SS 6.8.1)

The service owner ensures a service is managed with a business focus and is responsible to the customer for the initiation, transition and ongoing maintenance and support of a particular service. The service owner is also accountable to the IT director or service management director for the delivery of a specific IT service. Their accountability for a specific service within an organization is independent of where the underpinning technology components, processes or professional capabilities reside.

Service ownership is critical to service management and one person may fulfil the service owner role for more than one service. Key responsibilities include:

- Ensuring that the ongoing service delivery and support meet agreed customer requirements via effective service monitoring and performance
- Working with business relationship management to ensure that the service provider can meet customer requirements
- Ensuring consistent and appropriate communication with customers for service-related enquiries and issues
- Representing the service across the organization; for example, by attending change advisory board (CAB) meetings
- Serving as the point of escalation (notification) for major incidents relating to the service
- Participating in internal and external service review meetings
- Participating in negotiating SLAs and operational level agreements (OLAs) relating to the service
- Identifying opportunities for, and making, improvements to the service.

The service owner is responsible for continual improvement and the management of change affecting the service under their care. The service owner is a primary stakeholder in all of the underlying IT processes which enable or support the service they own.

1.5.5   The RACI model (SS 6.9)

Roles are accountable to, or responsible for, an activity. However, as services, processes and their component activities run through an entire organization, each activity must be clearly mapped to well-defined roles. To support this, the RACI model or 'authority matrix' can be used to define the roles and responsibilities in relation to processes and activities.

RACI is an acronym for:

- **Responsible** The person or people responsible for correct execution (i.e. for getting the job done)
- **Accountable** The person who has ownership of quality and the end result. Only one person can be accountable for each task
- **Consulted** The people who are consulted and whose opinions are sought. They have involvement through input of knowledge and information
- **Informed** The people who are kept up to date on progress. They receive information about process execution and quality.

Only one person should be accountable for any process or individual activity, although several people may be responsible for executing parts of the activity.

1.6   SERVICE OFFERINGS AND AGREEMENTS WITHIN THE CONTEXT OF THE SERVICE LIFECYCLE

1.6.1   SOA within the service lifecycle

Service offerings and agreements (SOA) starts at the centre of the service lifecycle. It concentrates on processes within service strategy and service design, and the links required between these processes to ensure the provision of high-quality services which provide true value in support of business needs and outcomes.

The SOA processes cannot be considered in isolation. These processes must be linked together and interface with other relevant lifecycle processes, with clearly defined interfaces, to manage, design, support and maintain services, IT infrastructures, environments, applications and data.

The processes detailed in this publication in support of SOA are as follows:

- Service portfolio management
- Service catalogue management
- Service level management
- Demand management
- Supplier management
- Financial management for IT services
- Business relationship management.

As well as understanding in depth the above processes it is necessary to have an appreciation of strategy management for IT services and design coordination.

Within SOA, the above processes are considered from the day-to-day operational perspective; aspects such as process implementation are considered within *ITIL Service Design* and *ITIL Service Strategy*.

1.6.2   Strategy management for IT services (SS 4.1.1–4.1.3)

Strategy management for IT services is the process which defines how the service strategy will form part of the overall enterprise strategy by maintaining the organization's perspective, position, plans and patterns for the provision of IT services and their management.

1.6.2.1   Purpose

The purpose of strategy management for IT services is to provide details of how the service provider can help an organization to achieve business outcomes. It does this by establishing mechanisms and criteria to determine which services best meet business outcomes and by defining efficient and effective service management processes that ensure the service strategy achieves its defined objectives.

1.6.2.2   Objectives

The objectives of strategy management for IT services are to:

- Analyse the internal and external environments in which the service provider exists
- Identify opportunities that will benefit the business
- Identify any constraints that may prevent business outcomes being achieved and define how these can be removed or reduced
- Agree on the service provider's perspective, then define a clear vision and mission for the service provider and review it regularly to ensure its continued relevance

- Establish the position of the service provider in relation to its customers and other service providers, including how to maintain a competitive advantage
- Produce and maintain strategic planning documents that are circulated to stakeholders and translated into tactical and operational plans to enable delivery of the strategy.

1.6.2.3   Scope

Strategy management is the responsibility of an organization's executives. It allows them to set organizational objectives and specify how these objectives will be met by prioritizing investments. The organization's strategy may be broken down into separate strategies for each business unit. Enterprise strategy management is responsible for linking the separate strategies to ensure overall consistency. The main focus for the service provider is to ensure the IT strategy, tactics and operations support and validate the business strategy objectives.

Note there is a difference between the service strategy and the ITSM strategy:

- **Service strategy** The strategy that a service provider will follow to define and execute services that meet a customer's business objectives. For an IT service provider the service strategy is a subset of the IT strategy.
- **ITSM strategy** The tactical plan for identifying, implementing and executing the processes used to manage services identified in the service strategy. In an IT service provider, the ITSM strategy is a subset of the service strategy.

1.6.2.4   Value to business

Without a strategy an organization will react to stakeholder demands but will fail to consider the overall impact on the organization. A well-defined and well-managed strategy ensures that resources and capabilities are aligned to achieve the business outcomes and that investments match the organization's intended development and growth.

For the service provider, strategy management ensures that the service portfolio contains a suitable set of services with a clearly defined and communicated purpose and roles.

For customers, strategy management allows them to clearly articulate their business priorities, enabling the service provider to make decisions on how they are best met, and to determine whether changes in IT strategy are needed.

1.6.3   Design coordination (SD 4.1.1–4.1.3)

1.6.3.1   Purpose

The purpose of design coordination is to ensure the goals and objectives of the service design stage are met by providing and maintaining a single point of coordination and control for all activities and processes within the service design lifecycle stage.

1.6.3.2   Objectives

The objectives of design coordination are:

- Ensure consistent design of appropriate services, service management information systems, architectures, technology and processes, aligned to meet current and evolving business outcomes
- Coordinate all design activities across projects, changes, suppliers and support teams, managing schedules, resources and conflicts as required
- Produce service design packages based on service charters and updates from change requests, and coordinate their handover to service transition

- Ensure the adoption of common frameworks, standards and re-usable design practices where appropriate, including service models and solutions that conform to all architectural, governance and strategic requirements
- Use service models and solutions to conform to the strategic requirements
- Monitor, plan, coordinate and manage the continual improvement and quality criteria for the service design lifecycle stages, including handover from service strategy, through service design activities and to service transition.

1.6.3.3   Scope

The design coordination process oversees design activity related to new and changed service solutions ready for transition into or retirement from the operational environment. The design coordination process may focus on projects and major changes that require extensive and complex design effort. Not all changes will require that level of rigour for success. The criterion for use of the design coordination process varies from organization to organization, focusing on business outcomes with minimal impacts and as little disruption to business operations as possible.

1.6.3.4   Value to business

Design coordination provides the desired business outcomes through the use of solution designs and service design packages to ensure consistent quality.

Design coordination ensures that:

- The intended business value of services is achieved through design at acceptable risk and cost
- Rework and unplanned costs in later lifecycle stages are kept to a minimum by paying attention to design prior to development

- The design conforms to a consistent service architecture that facilitates integration and data exchange between services and systems
- Improved service value, confidence, quality and agility are achieved through a design focus on satisfaction and outcomes for customers, users and the business.

1.6.4   Identification of customer requirements (SD 3.1.3, 3.4, 3.5)

New or changed business requirements are managed by the service provider's design process whereby the service solution is formulated and developed to meet the documented business needs.

There are five aspects of service design relating to new or changed services:

- Service solutions for new or changed services use the requirements detailed in the service portfolio. The solution is produced, validated and agreed against corporate and IT policies to ensure consistency with all existing services
- Management information systems and tools (including service portfolio) are reviewed to ensure they are capable of supporting the new or changed service
- Technology and management architectures are reviewed to ensure they are consistent and capable of maintaining and operating the new or changed service
- Processes are reviewed to ascertain whether the processes, roles, responsibilities and skills have the capability to operate, support and maintain the new or changed service; if not, they need to be enhanced

■ Measurement methods and metrics are reviewed to ascertain whether existing approaches are suitable for the new or changed service, or whether new measurement methods and metrics need to be developed.

1.6.4.1   Requirements identification

A holistic approach should be adopted for the design of all elements of a new service, its constituent components and their inter-relationships to meet all business requirements, including:

■ Service scalability to meet future business objectives
■ Supported business processes and units
■ IT service and business requirements for functionality (utility) and the service itself (warranty) as documented in service level requirements (SLRs) and SLAs
■ Technology components to deploy and deliver the service
■ Internal and external supporting services and their associated OLAs and underpinning contracts
■ Service performance measurements and metrics
■ Legislated and required security levels
■ Sustainability requirements for the service.

The impact of the new or changed service on the existing services should be considered and, if services are supplied by multiple providers, a central design authority should be established to ensure consistency. There are four technology domains that support services and need to be assessed: infrastructure; environment; data and information; and applications.

1.6.4.2   Business requirements and drivers (identification and documentation)

Accurate information is essential for the service provider to be able to understand the required service quality and business drivers; i.e. the people, information and tasks that are needed to support business objectives. Business information needs to be obtained and agreed in three main areas to maintain service alignment: existing, new, and retiring services.

A formal approach to the collection of the business information includes:

- Creation of a project using project management methodology and the appointment of a project manager and team
- Identification of all stakeholders with details of their requirements and the anticipated benefits
- Requirements analysis, prioritization, agreement and documentation
- Determination and agreement of outline budget and business benefits
- Agreement of corporate requirements and resolution of any potential business unit conflicts
- Sign-off process and the agreed procedures to handle requirement changes to reduce 'scope creep'
- Development of a customer engagement plan.

The business relationship management process plays a key role in these activities.

1.6.5 Customer perception of value, utility and warranty (SS 3.2.3–3.2.4)

1.6.5.1 Value

The value of a service is driven by how it matches the customer's expectations and this influences what the customer is willing to pay irrespective of its cost. A service does not have an intrinsic value; it relies on what it enables someone to do. Consequently, value is determined by the person receiving the service.

The characteristics of value are:

- Defined by customers
- Affordable mix of features
- Achieves objectives
- Changes over time and according to circumstances.

Services will be valued by an organization if their perceived worth outweighs the cost. In order to appreciate the value of IT, the customer should consider:

- What service(s) did IT provide?
- What did the service(s) achieve?
- How much did the service(s) cost or what price was charged?

Calculating the value of services can be linked in part to tangible business outcomes. However, there is more to value creation than the function of a service and its cost.

The three areas that determine value are business outcomes, customer preferences and customer perceptions. Customer perceptions need to be understood in order to enable the service provider to influence the customer's perceived value. Engaging with the customer enables the service provider to determine where effort can be concentrated in order to cost-effectively increase the perceived value and realized business outcomes of the service to the customer.

A marketing mindset is required in order to view the service from the perspective of the customer. Questions to be considered include: What is our business? Who is our customer? What does the customer value? Who depends on our services? How do they use our services? Why are they valuable to them? The answers to these questions enable service providers to understand the customer context and differentiate their offerings.

1.6.5.2   Utility and warranty

A combination of utility (fitness for purpose) and warranty (fitness for use) enables the delivery of services that provide value to the organization. Services must satisfy both utility and warranty requirements to deliver value and fulfil business objectives. A service that provides utility but fails to deliver warranty, or vice versa, will fail to deliver successful outcomes and business value.

In many organizations, where development is separated from operations, the initial focus is on delivering the utility of a service, ensuring it provides the functionality required to support the business operation at the right cost. Warranty aspects are ignored, assuming manageability is being taken care of. In fact warranty needs to be designed and built together with utility. Failure to do this can result in a limited ability to deliver the utility and it can be expensive and disruptive to design warranty after a service has been deployed.

When the correct balance of utility and warranty has been achieved, it is recommended that consideration is given to both aspects during initial service design, and how each will contribute to the ultimate value of the service when in live operation.

2 Service portfolio management

2.1 PURPOSE AND OBJECTIVES (SS 4.2.1)

The purpose of service portfolio management (SPM) is to ensure that the service provider has the right mix of services to balance the investment in IT with the ability to meet business outcomes. It tracks the investment in services throughout their lifecycle and works with other service management processes to ensure that the appropriate returns are being achieved. It ensures that services are clearly defined and linked to the achievement of business outcomes, thereby making sure that all design, transition and operation activities are aligned with the value of the services.

The objectives of SPM are to:

■ Provide a process and mechanisms to enable an organization to investigate and decide on which services to provide
■ Maintain the definitive portfolio of services provided, articulating the business needs each service meets and the business outcomes it supports
■ Provide a mechanism for the organization to evaluate how services enable it to achieve its strategy, and respond to changes in its internal or external environments
■ Control which services are offered, under what conditions and at what level of investment
■ Track the investment in services throughout their lifecycle
■ Analyse which services are no longer viable and when they should be retired.

2.2   SCOPE (SS 4.2.2)

The scope of SPM includes all services planned for the future, currently delivered and withdrawn from service. The primary concern is the value generated from the services, so SPM tracks investments in services and compares them with the desired business outcomes.

Internal service providers work with the organization's business units to link services to business outcomes and to compare investment with returns. External service providers use the revenue generated; when this is achieved efficiently it will facilitate profitability.

SPM evaluates the value of services throughout their lifecycle, and must be able to compare what newer services have offered with the retired services they have replaced. SPM plays an important role in all stages of the service lifecycle.

2.3   VALUE TO THE BUSINESS (SS 4.2.3)

SPM enables the business to make sound decisions about investments. Services are implemented only if there is a good business case demonstrating a clear return on investment (ROI). SPM compares the customer's expected outcomes with the investment required to build and deliver the service.

Customers understand what the service provider will deliver to them and under what conditions, enabling them to make investment decisions and evaluate additional opportunities. SPM can be a tool for innovation for the organization.

The service provider can equip its customers to build their strategies, as long as it provides what it has promised.

2.4   POLICIES, PRINCIPLES AND BASIC CONCEPTS (SS 4.2.4)

SPM ensures that the service provider has an understanding of all the services that it provides, including the investments, strategy, and objectives required for each service, before it makes tactical plans for how to manage those services. SPM plays a role in strategy generation, and follows through the service lifecycle to ensure that the agreed strategy is appropriately executed at each stage.

This approach serves two purposes:

- It prevents mis-steps, such as performing a tool selection before optimizing processes
- It ensures continuity between the high-level intent and the detailed-level execution.

For IT services, the SPM approach helps managers prioritize investments and improve the allocation of resources. Changes to portfolios are governed by policies and procedures. Portfolios instil the financial discipline necessary to avoid making investments that will not yield value.

When services in the catalogue are phased out or retired, the related knowledge and information are stored in a knowledge base for future use.

2.4.1   Service portfolio

A service portfolio describes a provider's services in terms of business value, articulating business needs and the provider's response to those needs. As the basis for a decision framework, a service portfolio clarifies or helps to clarify the following strategic questions:

- Why should a customer buy these services?
- Why should a customer buy these services from us?
- What are the pricing or chargeback models?
- What are our strengths and weaknesses, priorities and risks?
- How should our resources and capabilities be allocated?

The service portfolio represents the investment made in an organization's services, and also articulates the value that services help it to realize.

The service portfolio is divided into three phases: service pipeline (proposed or in development), service catalogue (live or available for deployment) and retired services (see Figure 2.1).

The service portfolio provides:

- The complete set of services managed by a service provider
- Identification of services at a conceptual stage (those that could be provided if resources, capabilities and funding are available)
- An understanding of the opportunity costs of the existing portfolio and better fiscal discipline
- Information for the service provider to assess what it should continue to do and where it should reallocate resources and capabilities.

The service portfolio represents all the resources presently engaged or being released in various phases of the service lifecycle. This is a very important governance aspect of SPM. Entry, progress and exit are approved only with agreed funding and a financial plan for recovering costs or showing profit as necessary. The service portfolio should have the right mix of services in the pipeline and catalogue to secure the financial viability of the service provider.

Figure 2.1 The service portfolio and its contents

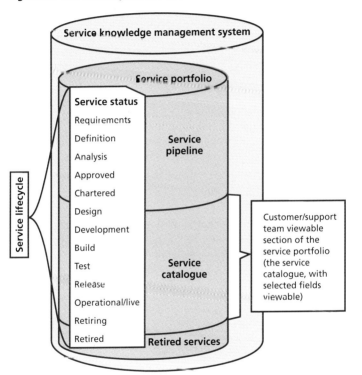

SPM is responsible for managing the service portfolio. This includes being responsible for defining which services will be entered into the service portfolio and how those services are tracked and progressed, thereby ensuring that the services provided contribute to strategic objectives and meet the agreed business outcomes.

2.4.2 Service pipeline

The service pipeline provides a business view of all services and investment opportunities that are under consideration or development, but are not yet available to customers. This part of the service portfolio it is not normally published to customers.

There are many ways in which a service can enter the service pipeline; for example:

- A customer requests a new service
- New opportunities are identified from the service provider's strategy, the customer's business or new technology
- The business outcome is underserved by current services
- Service management processes (capacity management, service level management or problem management) identify a better solution than the services that are currently offered
- Continual service improvement processes identify a gap in the current service portfolio.

Sometimes customer access is permitted to the service pipeline for services in which they are directly involved. However, in many cases direct access is not necessary; the information is just used to provide the customer with updates. When the service is moved from development to operational, it transfers from the service pipeline to the service catalogue.

2.4.3   Service catalogue

The service catalogue holds information on all live IT services and is the only part of the service portfolio that is published to the customers. Items can enter the service catalogue only after due diligence has been performed on related costs and risks. Resources are engaged to fully support active services.

The service catalogue consists of services that are active in the service operation phase and those that have been approved to be offered to current or prospective customers. It provides a mechanism for service order and demand channelling. Thus it acts as an acquisition portal for customers, with pricing, contact points, service-level commitments and terms and conditions for service provisioning.

There may be multiple service catalogues as they articulate the services provider's operational capability within the context of a customer or market space. The service catalogue is used as a tool to aid SPM decision-making. It does this by linking service assets, services and business outcomes and also by providing information on the demand for services.

A subset of the service catalogue may be third-party or outsourced services that are offered to customers with varying levels of value addition or combination with other catalogue items.

2.4.4   Retired services

Depending on the organization, services are designated as retired either when they are no longer available to new customers but are still being delivered to existing customers, or when the service is no longer being delivered.

Retired services are kept in the service portfolio to provide a fall-back position in case the replacement service fails to meet the requirements. Often regulatory requirements dictate the retention time and maintenance of retired services and archived data.

2.4.5 Other areas

SPM relies on other areas, including:

- **Configuration management system** This records and controls configuration data
- **Application portfolio** Entries should all be linked to one or more entries in the service portfolio
- **Customer portfolio** Ensure the relationship between business outcomes, customers and services is well understood
- **Customer agreement portfolio** An intersection of the service and customer portfolios, usually managed as part of SPM
- **Project portfolio** Helps to track the status of projects and provides financial and progress information on multiple projects that are required to develop and deliver new services
- **Service models** For impact analysis of new or changed services.

SPM also contributes to market spaces and service growth by aligning service assets, services and business outcomes.

2.5   PROCESS ACTIVITIES, METHODS AND TECHNIQUES (SS 4.2.5)

SPM consists of four main phases of activity:

- **Define** Creates an inventory of new and existing services, ensures business cases and validates portfolio data

- **Analyse** Performs an analysis of services to indicate whether the service can optimize value and how to balance and prioritize supply and demand
- **Approve** Authorizes the level of investment required to ensure that sufficient resources are funded to deliver the anticipated levels of service
- **Charter** Authorizes the project, stating the scope and terms of reference. Communicates the decisions made, allocates the resources and charters the services.

2.5.1   Process initiation

Once the service portfolio has been created all new and changed services will go through a formal process of assessment and approval. A variety of sources provide information on the new and changed services. Therefore SPM needs to maintain a central record of all plans, request and suggestions.

2.5.2   Define

'Define' captures details of the desired business outcomes, opportunities, utility and warranty requirements and the services themselves together with the anticipated investment. At this stage the new or changed service is approved and enters the design stage.

The areas to be considered during 'define' include:

- **Strategy** The strategic plans, identified market spaces and outcomes, priorities and policies submitted to SPM.
- **Requests from business** These are received in many formats, registered, and updates on the request status are provided. Standard methods and formats for recording should be used.

- **Service improvement opportunities and plans** Information is required on improvements relating to people, process tools as well as changes to services.
- **Service suggestions** Details of any suggestions that require investment over a predetermined threshold, or any changes that affect agreed utility and warranty levels, need to be included.
- **Existing services** These are recorded and brought under formal service management control; duplication of services should be avoided.
- **Service, business and customer outcomes** Expected outcomes are captured without the constraints imposed by existing technology.
- **Service model** A high-level view of how the service components fit together and the boundaries of the potential service is documented.
- **Impact on service portfolio** The impact is evaluated for existing utility, warranty and investment on existing services within the service portfolio.
- **Impact on service model** The impact is evaluated on the existing service model.

2.5.3 Analyse

The analysis of each service moving through the SPM process is performed by linking it to the service strategy.

Questions that help to translate the organization's strategic intent for services include:

- What are the long-term goals of the service organization?
- What services are required to meet those goals?

- What capabilities and resources are required for the organization to achieve those services?
- How will we get there?

SPM articulates how the perspective, position, plan and patterns will be translated into actual services. The answers guide the analysis and the desired outcomes of SPM, and require the involvement of senior leaders and subject matter experts.

The way in which services are analysed needs to be clearly defined before the analysis actually begins. The analysis phase requires input from several specialist areas. To facilitate this some organizations use a standard pool of senior architects and managers; this is known as the service architecture board. This group also validates the analysis work and ensures that the change proposal is properly prepared.

The analysis phase includes activities that review the service portfolio on an ongoing basis and work with financial management for IT services to quantify the investments and value for each service.

A useful tool for making decisions on the timing and sequencing of investments in a service portfolio is an option space tool; see Figure 2.2. An option space can guide decisions on where and when to invest. In addition to financial measures, other factors may also influence investment decisions. These include mission imperatives, compliance, trends, intangible benefits, strategic or business fit, social responsibilities and innovation.

Figure 2.2 The option space tool for IT service management

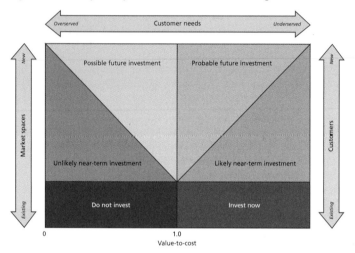

When prioritizing investments, service investments are normally split between three strategic categories:

- **Run the business (RTB)** Investments centred on maintaining service operations
- **Grow the business (GTB)** Investments intended to grow the organization's scope of services
- **Transform the business (TTB)** Investments to move into new market spaces.

Investment categories are further divided into the following budget allocations:

- **Venture** Create services in a new market space
- **Growth** Create new services in existing market space

- **Discretionary** Provide enhancements to existing services
- **Non-discretionary** Maintain existing services
- **Core** Maintain business-critical services.

Termination of services can be a potentially large hidden cost for a service provider. A clear path is required for retiring redundant services. Since the cost of retiring a service may temporarily exceed that of maintaining it, its budget allocation can shift from non-discretionary to discretionary.

On completion of the analysis the results are formatted and documented in a business case.

2.5.4 Approve

In this phase approvals (with the corresponding authorization for new services and resources) or disapprovals of the future state take place. The decisions about how services can be progressed through the SPM process fall into six categories:

- **Retain or build** Services that are aligned with and relevant to the organization's strategy.
- **Replace** Services that do not meet minimum levels of technical and functional fitness.
- **Rationalize** Services that are composed of multiple releases of the same operating system, multiple versions of the same software and/or multiple versions of system platforms providing similar functions by removing duplication.
- **Refactor** Services that meet the technical and functional criteria of the organization but display unclear process or system boundaries. Services can be refactored to include only the core functionality, with common services providing the remainder or where they have embedded re-usable services.

- **Renew** Services that meet functional fitness criteria, but fail on technical fitness.
- **Retire** Services that do not meet minimum levels of technical and functional fitness.

2.5.5 Charter

The service charter ensures there is a common understanding of what will be built and the associated costs and timeframes. The contents of the charter cover an overview, the approach and project authority for the service. It is important that communication with the stakeholders on project progress is maintained.

The service charter contains details of the scope and requirements of the project. It is used to initiate the work of design and transition and it remains active throughout. SPM receives progress updates which are captured in the service portfolio and are used to track changes to the estimated cost or capability. Any significant differences are escalated to the stakeholders.

2.6   TRIGGERS, INPUTS, OUTPUTS AND INTERFACES (SS 4.2.6)

The main triggers for SPM are changes to strategy and services (existing or new). Other triggers can include identified changes to estimates (design); failure to meet expected business outcomes (operation); cost escalation (design, operation); and service improvement initiatives.

Inputs include:

- Strategy plans and service improvement opportunities
- Financial reports

- Requests, suggestions or complaints from the business
- Project updates for services at charter stage.

Outputs include:

- Up-to-date service portfolio and service charters
- Status reports on new or changed services
- Reports on investment in services and ROI
- Change proposals and identified risks

Interfaces include:

- **Service catalogue management** The catalogue is part of the service portfolio
- **Strategy management for IT services** Guidance on the types of services to be included in the portfolio
- **Financial management for IT services** Information and tools for ROI and cost tracking
- **Demand management** Information on patterns of business activity to determine service utilization
- **Business relationship management** Initiates requests, obtains information and business requirements, and updates customers on the status of services within the service portfolio
- **Service design processes** Service level, capacity, availability, IT service continuity, information security and supplier management provide the information required for the creation of successful services
- **Service transition processes** Change management, service asset and configuration management, service validation and testing, and knowledge management provide control, coordination and validation of services before they move into live operation

- **Continual service improvement** Provides feedback on the actual use and value of services, allowing comparison with what was anticipated.

2.7   INFORMATION MANAGEMENT (SS 4.2.7)

SPM uses databases or structured documents to manage the information required. These documents include the service portfolio, project portfolio, application portfolio, customer portfolio and customer agreement portfolio. Service models are used to understand the composition of proposed services and are supported by the use of a configuration management system. Information from the service strategy enables SPM to define the mix of services required to best meet the organization's strategic objectives.

2.8   CRITICAL SUCCESS FACTORS AND KEY PERFORMANCE INDICATORS (SS 4.2.8)

The efficiency and effectiveness of the process can be measured by identifying critical success factors (CSFs) for the process, each CSF being supported by key performance indicators (KPIs):

- **CSF** Formal process to investigate and decide on which services to provide:
    - **KPI** A formal SPM process exists, owned by SPM process owner
    - **KPI** SPM is audited and reviewed annually and meets its objectives
- **CSF** Ability to document each service provided including its business needs and business outcomes:
    - **KPI** An audited service portfolio of all services exists, used as a basis for deciding which services to offer

- **KPI** A documented process for defining business need and outcome exists, owned by SPM process owner
- **KPI** Each service in the service portfolio has at least one business outcome
■ **CSF** Formal process to review whether services are enabling the organization to achieve its strategy:
  - **KPI** SPM provides regular and structured feedback to strategy management for IT services regarding the performance of each service and its ability to meet stated business outcomes
  - **KPI** An audit of strategy documents and the service portfolio shows that the business outcomes in the service portfolio are consistent with those stated in the relevant strategy
■ **CSF** Ability to change services in response to changes in the internal and external environments:
  - **KPI** Every environmental change identified in strategy management for IT services has a service portfolio entry that has been evaluated and a decision has been made about the need for change to relevant services
  - **KPI** A review of the organization's strategy shows that services in the service portfolio continue to meet all changed business objectives and outcomes
  - **KPI** Customer surveys show continued high levels of satisfaction
■ **CSF** Tools that enable the service provider to track the investment in services throughout their lifecycle:
  - **KPI** The investment in each service is quantified in the service portfolio
  - **KPI** Investment in each service is reported, starting with the initial investment, and followed by monthly, quarterly or annual reports on ongoing investment

   – **KPI** The investments made are consistent with the projected ROI forecasts.

2.9   CHALLENGES AND RISKS (SS 4.2.9)

Challenges include:

- **Lack of access to customer and business information** This prevents SPM from understanding the desired business outcomes and strategies.
- **Lack of a formal project management approach** It is more difficult to charter services and track them through the design and transition stages.
- **Lack of a project portfolio** It is more difficult to assess the impact of new initiatives on new services or proposed changes to services.
- **Lack of a customer portfolio or customer agreement portfolio** This makes it difficult to identify the objectives, use and ROI for services.
- **A service portfolio that is focused only on the service provider aspects of services** It is difficult to calculate the value of services, model future utilization or validate the customer requirements for the service.
- **Lack of a formal change management process** This impacts the ability to control the introduction of new services, or manage changes to existing services.

Risks include:

- **Offering services without validated or complete information** Pressure from customers to offer a service means the decision is rushed, and SPM has not completed a full investigation of the risks associated with the service.

■ **Offering services without defining how they will be measured** It is difficult to calculate the ROI of the services without a clear value proposition. Where cost-cutting is being considered, service providers may eliminate apparently valuable services for which no tangible returns can be demonstrated.

2.10   ROLES AND RESPONSIBILITIES (SS 6.8.7)

2.10.1 Service portfolio management process owner
■ Carrying out the generic process owner role for SPM (see section 1.5); working with other process owners to ensure there is an integrated approach to the design and implementation of SPM.

2.10.2 Service portfolio management process manager
■ Carrying out the generic process manager role for SPM (see section 1.5)
■ Managing and maintaining the organization's service portfolio
■ Managing the surrounding processes for keeping the portfolio attractive to customers and up to date
■ Marketing the portfolio, and in particular the service catalogue
■ Helping to formulate service packages and associated options to meet customers' needs.

3 Service catalogue management

3.1 PURPOSE AND OBJECTIVES (SD 4.2.1)

The purpose of service catalogue management is to provide a single source of consistent information on all agreed services (either operational or in preparation to be run operationally) and to ensure that it is widely available to those who are approved to access it.

The main objective of service catalogue management is to manage the information contained within the service catalogue, ensuring it is accurate and reflects the current details, status, interfaces and dependencies of all services that are being run, or are being prepared to run, in the live environment. Other objectives are to ensure that the service catalogue information is available to support those with approved access, that it meets the evolving needs of all of the service management processes and that it includes the provision of interface and dependency information.

3.2 SCOPE (SD 4.2.2)

The scope of service catalogue management is to provide and maintain accurate information on all services that are being transitioned or have been transitioned into the live environment.

Activities in scope include:

- Definition of services and service packages
- Development and maintenance of appropriate service and service package descriptions
- Production and maintenance of an accurate service catalogue

- Management of interfaces, dependencies and consistency between the service catalogue and service portfolio
- Management of interfaces and dependencies between all services and supporting services within the service catalogue and the configuration management system (CMS)
- Management of interfaces and dependencies between all services, and supporting components and configuration items (CIs) within the service catalogue and the CMS

3.3   VALUE TO THE BUSINESS (SD 4.2.3)

The service catalogue is a central source of information on the IT services delivered by the service provider organization, providing all areas of the business with an accurate, consistent view of the IT services, their details and status. It contains a customer-facing view of the IT services in use, how they are intended to be used, the business processes they enable, and the levels and quality of service the customer can expect for each service.

Service catalogue management allows organizations to:

- Utilize the service catalogue to promote common understanding of the IT services and improve the relationship between the customer and service provider
- Provide a correlation between service provider activities and service assets, business outcomes and processes, improving the service provider focus on customer outcomes
- Use service catalogue information to improve efficiency and effectiveness of all service management processes
- Manage interfaces, dependencies and maintain consistency between the service catalogue and service portfolio.

3.4 POLICIES, PRINCIPLES AND BASIC CONCEPTS (SD 4.2.4, SS 4.2.4.3, SD APPENDIX G)

Once a service is 'chartered' (i.e. being developed for use by customers), service design produces the specifications for the service and development of the service catalogue entry begins. The service catalogue contains a summary of each service, its characteristics and details of its customers and maintainers.

A CMS or asset database can provide valuable sources of information, which need to be verified before they can be included within either the service portfolio or service catalogue.

Figure 3.1 gives examples of the contents of a service portfolio and service catalogue.

A policy is required for both the portfolio and catalogue, stating the services to be recorded within them. Service details, together with the service status, are recorded for each service. The policy also details the responsibilities and scope for each constituent section of the portfolio.

The organization needs to develop a policy stating what a service is and how it is defined and agreed internally.

When service providers have many customers or serve many businesses, many service catalogues may be projected from the service portfolio.

There may be two layers of services in the service catalogue; one shows the customer-facing services while the other, which is not usually seen by the customer, shows the underpinning supporting services.

*Figure 3.1 Example elements of a service portfolio and
service catalogue*

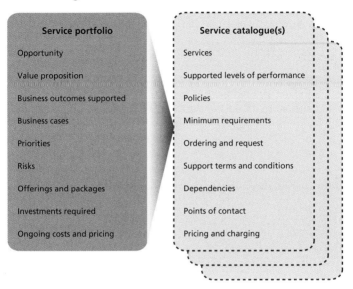

Service portfolio	Service catalogue(s)
Opportunity	Services
Value proposition	Supported levels of performance
Business outcomes supported	Policies
Business cases	Minimum requirements
Priorities	Ordering and request
Risks	Support terms and conditions
Offerings and packages	Dependencies
Investments required	Points of contact
Ongoing costs and pricing	Pricing and charging

3.5   PROCESS ACTIVITIES, METHODS AND
TECHNIQUES (SD 4.2.5)

Key activities in the service catalogue management process include:

■ Agreeing and documenting a service definition with all
relevant parties
■ Interfacing with service portfolio management (SPM) to agree
the contents of the service portfolio and service catalogue

- Producing and maintaining a service catalogue, in conjunction with the service portfolio
- Interfacing with business and IT service continuity management to identify and manage the dependencies of business units and their business processes on the supporting IT services contained in the business service catalogue
- Interfacing with support teams, suppliers and service asset and configuration management to identify the interfaces and dependencies between IT services and supporting services, components and CIs in the service catalogue
- Interfacing with business relationship management and service level management to ensure that information is aligned with the business and business processes.

3.6   TRIGGERS, INPUTS, OUTPUTS AND INTERFACES (SD 4.2.6)

Triggers for service catalogue management are changes in business requirements and services. Therefore key triggers are requests for change (RFCs) and the change management process, including new services, changes to existing services or services being retired.

Inputs include:

- Business information from an organization's business and IT strategy, plans and financial plans, and information on its current and future requirements from the service portfolio
- Business impact analysis, providing information on the impact, priority and risk associated with each service or changes to requirements
- Details of any agreed, new or changed business requirements from the service portfolio

- Service portfolio and all related data and documents
- The CMS and RFCs
- Feedback from all other processes.

Outputs include:

- Documentation and agreement of a definition of the service
- Updates to the service portfolio, including current status of all services and requirements for services
- Updates to RFCs
- The service catalogue, including details, current status, interfaces and dependencies for all live services and those being transitioned into the live environment.

Interfaces include:

- **SPM** Determines the services to be chartered and moved to the service catalogue, and defines the critical service information
- **Business relationship management** Ensures clear definition of how the service meets the customer's needs
- **Demand management** Determines the composition of service packages and ensures that these packages are appropriately represented in the service catalogue
- **Service level management** The service catalogue reflects the negotiated specific levels of service warranty to be delivered.

3.7   INFORMATION MANAGEMENT (SD 4.2.7)

The service catalogue is the main repository for information. It must therefore be accurate and updated through the change management process. The catalogue can be in many forms, including via an intranet, a specialist tool or part of an integrated service management suite. The physical implementation can range from one to multiple repositories.

The catalogue can support many differing views depending on the audience for the information. Integration with the service portfolio is critical as well as access to other related areas such as service level agreements (SLAs) and the facility for service requests.

3.8   CRITICAL SUCCESS FACTORS AND KEY PERFORMANCE INDICATORS (SD 4.2.8)

The efficiency and effectiveness of the process can be measured by identifying critical success factors (CSFs) for the process, each CSF being supported by key performance indicators (KPIs):

- **CSF** An accurate service catalogue:
    - **KPI** Increase in the number of services recorded and managed within the service catalogue as a percentage of those being delivered and transitioned into the live environment
    - **KPI** Percentage reduction in the number of variances detected between the information contained within the service catalogue and the 'real world' situation
- **CSF** Business users' awareness of the services being provided:
    - **KPI** Percentage increase in business user survey responses showing knowledge of services listed in the service catalogue
    - **KPI** Increase in measured business user access to intranet-based service catalogue
- **CSF** IT staff awareness of the technology-supporting services:
    - **KPI** Percentage increase in completeness of supporting services against IT components that make up those services

- **KPI** Increase in service desk and other IT staff having access to information to support all live services, measured by the percentage of incidents with the appropriate service-related information.

3.9   CHALLENGES AND RISKS (SD 4.2.9)

The major challenge facing service catalogue management is maintaining an accurate service catalogue as part of a service portfolio, incorporating all catalogue views as part of an overall CMS and service knowledge management system (SKMS).

The risks associated with providing an accurate service catalogue include:

- Data in the catalogue being inaccurate and not under rigorous change control
- Poor acceptance of the service catalogue and its usage in all operational processes. The more active the catalogue is, the more likely it is to be accurate
- Inaccuracy of service information from the business, IT and service portfolio
- Lack of tools and resources required to maintain the information
- Poor access to accurate change management information and processes
- Poor access to, and support of, appropriate and up-to-date CMS and SKMS
- Circumvention of use of the service portfolio and service catalogue
- Information that is either too detailed to maintain accurately or too high-level to be of value.

3.10   ROLES AND RESPONSIBILITIES (SD 6.3.6)

3.10.1 Service catalogue management process owner

■ Carrying out the generic process owner role for the service catalogue management process (see section 1.5)

■ Working with other process owners to ensure an integrated approach to the design and implementation of service catalogue, service portfolio, service level, and business relationship management.

3.10.2 Service catalogue management process manager

■ Carrying out the generic process manager role for the service catalogue management process (see section 1.5)

■ Coordinating interfaces with other processes, including service asset and configuration management and release and deployment management

■ Recording the services that are being prepared for operation and all operational services in the service catalogue, ensuring views are maintained and available

■ Ensuring that all information in the catalogue is adequately protected, up to date and consistent with the service portfolio.

4   Service level management

Service level management (SLM) is a vital process, responsible for agreeing and documenting service level targets and responsibilities within service level agreements (SLAs) and service level requirements (SLRs) for every service and related activity within IT. Ensuring that targets are appropriate and reflect business requirements means that the service delivered will align with business needs and meet the service quality expectations of the customers and users.

The SLA is effectively a level of assurance or warranty with regard to the level of service quality delivered by the service provider for each of the services delivered to the business. The success of SLM depends on the quality of the service portfolio and the service catalogue contents.

4.1   PURPOSE AND OBJECTIVES (SD 4.3.1)

The purpose of SLM is to ensure that all current and planned IT services are delivered to agreed organizational targets. This is accomplished through a constant cycle of negotiating, agreeing, monitoring, reporting on and reviewing IT service targets and achievements, and through instigation of actions to correct or improve the level of service.

The objectives of SLM are to:

- Define, document, agree, monitor, measure, report and review the level of IT services provided
- Provide and improve relationships and communication with the business and customers
- Ensure specific and measurable targets are developed for all IT services

- Monitor and improve customer satisfaction with the quality of services delivered
- Ensure IT and customers have a clear and unambiguous expectation of the level of service to be delivered
- Ensure proactive measures to improve levels of service delivered are implemented, wherever cost-justifiable.

4.2   SCOPE (SD 4.3.2)

SLM includes:

- Cooperation with the business relationship management process, including development of relationships with the business as needed to achieve the SLM process objectives
- Negotiation and agreement of current and future requirements and targets, and the documentation and management of SLRs and SLAs for all operational services
- Development and management of appropriate operational level agreements (OLAs), ensuring alignment with SLAs
- Review of underpinning supplier contracts and agreements with supplier management, ensuring alignment with SLAs
- Proactive prevention of service failures, reduction of service risks and improvements in service quality, in conjunction with all other processes
- Reporting on and management of services and review of SLA breaches and weaknesses
- Periodic review, renewal and/or revision of SLAs, service scope and OLAs as appropriate
- Identification, review, prioritization of improvement opportunities for inclusion in the continual service improvement (CSI) register

■ Instigation and coordination of a service improvement plan (SIP) for the management, planning and implementation of all service and process improvements.

4.3   VALUE TO THE BUSINESS (SD 4.3.3)

SLM provides a consistent interface with the business for all service-related issues. Where targets are breached, SLM provides feedback on the cause and details the actions taken to prevent recurrence.

SLM provides a reliable communication channel and a trusted relationship with customer and business representatives.

4.4   POLICIES, PRINCIPLES AND BASIC CONCEPTS (SD 4.3.4, SD APPENDIX F)

SLM includes the planning, coordinating, drafting, agreeing, monitoring and reporting of SLAs, and the ongoing review of service achievements to ensure that the required and cost-justifiable service quality is maintained and gradually improved.

The service provider should establish clear policies for the SLM process; these include the minimum contents of the SLAs and OLAs, and how and when the agreements are renewed or renegotiated.

An SLA is a written agreement between an IT service provider and customer. It defines the key service targets and warranty elements and describes the utility and responsibilities of both parties. Details may include:

■ Service description
■ Scope of the agreement
■ Service hours

- Service availability (warranty)
- Reliability
- Customer support
- Contact points and escalation
- Service performance and capacity (warranty)
- Change management
- Service continuity (warranty)
- Security (warranty)
- Charging (if applicable)
- Service reporting and reviewing.

SLM is responsible for ensuring that all targets and measures agreed in SLAs with the business are supported by underpinning OLAs or contracts with internal support units and external partners or suppliers.

An OLA is an agreement between an IT service provider and another part of the same organization that assists with service provision. An OLA contains targets that underpin those within an SLA to ensure that targets are not breached by failure of a supporting activity. An OLA typically comprises:

- Support service description
- Scope of the agreement
- Service hours
- Service targets
- Contact points and escalation
- Service desk and incident response times and responsibilities
- Problem response times and responsibilities
- Change management
- Release and deployment management
- Service asset and configuration management
- Information security management

- Availability management
- IT service continuity management
- Capacity management
- Supplier management.

SLRs are customer requirements for an aspect of an IT service. They are based on business objectives and are used to negotiate agreed service level targets.

When an IT service provider engages a third-party supplier, clear and unambiguous expectations are required to ensure that the SLAs can be supported. These are expressed within contracts and agreements; in the case of a contract the agreement is legally binding.

4.5 PROCESS ACTIVITIES, METHODS AND TECHNIQUES (SD 4.3.5)

The interfaces between the main activities are illustrated in Figure 4.1.

4.5.1 Design SLA frameworks

Use the service catalogue to aid the design of an SLA structure. This ensures that all services and customers are covered to meet the organization's needs. Options include:

- **Service-based SLA** Covering all customers of that service. Multiple classes of service (for example, gold, silver and bronze) can increase the effectiveness of service-based SLAs.
- **Customer-based SLA** With an individual customer group, covering all the services they use. Only one signatory is normally required.

Figure 4.1 The service level management process

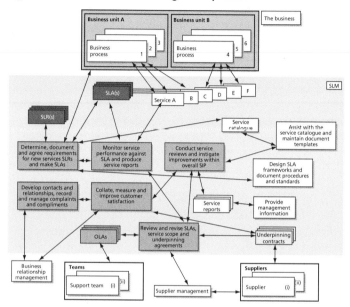

- **Combination of the above structures** Providing that all services and customers are covered, with no overlap or duplication.
- **Multi-level SLAs** For example, a three-layer structure: corporate level for all customers; customer level covering all services relevant to a particular business unit, regardless of the service being used; and service level relevant to a specific service for a specific customer group.

4.5.2 Determining, documenting and agreeing requirements for new services and producing SLRs

When the service catalogue has been produced and the SLA structure has been agreed, draft an initial SLR. Involve customers from the outset. Establish procedures for agreeing SLRs for new services being developed or procured.

SLRs need to be included in the service design criteria because they form part of the testing and trialling criteria as the service progresses through the stages of design and development or procurement.

The initial requirements may not be those ultimately agreed. Several iterations of negotiations may be required before an acceptable balance is struck between what is sought and what is achievable and affordable.

For new services being introduced into the live environment, undertake the planning and formalization of the support arrangements for the service. Define specific responsibilities and add them to existing contracts and OLAs, or agree new ones.

Where appropriate, complete initial training, familiarization and knowledge transfer for the service desk and other support groups before live support is needed.

4.5.3 Negotiating, documenting and agreeing SLAs for operational services

Before a new or changed service is accepted into live operation, an SLA is agreed, detailing the service level targets to be achieved and specifying the responsibilities of both the IT service provider and the customer.

If no existing SLAs are in place, monitoring, measuring and reporting on the current levels of service being delivered can provide information to inform negotiations with customers to establish acceptable targets.

Using the SLRs or other information from the customer about the required service levels, develop a pilot or draft SLA alongside the service itself. This can be gradually refined, formalized and then signed before the service is introduced into live use.

The SLA is signed by the appropriate managers on the customer and IT service provider sides to give a firm commitment by both parties.

Ensure awareness of SLAs and OLAs is cascaded to the service desk and other support groups.

4.5.4   Monitoring service performance against SLA

Only include items in an SLA that can be effectively monitored and measured at a commonly agreed point. Inclusion of items that cannot be effectively monitored often leads to disputes and loss of faith in SLM.

Existing monitoring capabilities need to be reviewed and upgraded as necessary, either before or in parallel with the drafting of SLAs, so that monitoring can help with the validation of proposed targets.

Ensure any incident- or problem-handling targets included in SLAs are reflected in the service desk tools and that they are used for escalation and monitoring purposes.

Transaction response times can be difficult to monitor, so consider either including a statement in the SLA to indicate the acceptable time beyond which it is reported to the service desk, or implementing automated client or server response time monitoring.

4.5.5   Producing service reports

SLA reporting mechanisms, intervals and report formats must be defined and agreed with the customers and synchronized with the reviewing cycle. Circulate reports in advance of the service level review meetings, so that any queries or disagreements can be resolved before the meeting.

Periodic reports detail performance against all SLA targets, together with details of any trends or specific actions being undertaken to improve service quality.

Reports need to reflect the customer's perception of service quality. Information needs to be accurate and to have been analysed and collated into concise and comprehensive reports on service performance against agreed business targets.

Reports can be time-consuming and effort-intensive to produce, so identify specific reporting needs and automate reporting as far as possible.

4.5.6   Conducting service reviews and instigating improvements within an overall SIP

Periodic review meetings must be held on a regular basis with customers to review the service achievement in the last period and to preview any issues for the coming period. The frequency and format of service review meetings must be agreed with the customers. Regular intervals are recommended; for example, monthly or quarterly.

Action must be placed on the customer or provider, as appropriate, to improve weak areas where targets are not being met. Minute the actions to be taken and review what progress has been made at the next meeting.

For any breach of service level, determine the cause of service loss and what can be done to prevent any recurrence. It may be necessary to review, renegotiate and agree different service targets, including any underpinning agreement or OLA.

Analyse the cost and impact of service breaches for input into and justification of SIP activities and actions. Report on the progress and success of the SIP.

4.5.7   Collate, measure and improve customer satisfaction

Manage customers' expectations by setting appropriate targets in the first place, and manage their ongoing expectations.

Where charges are being made for the services provided, these should modify customer demands. Otherwise use the support of senior business managers to ensure that excessive or unrealistic demands are not made.

Methods of monitoring customer perception include periodic questionnaires and customer surveys, feedback from service review meetings and post-implementation reviews, telephone perception surveys, user group or forum meetings and analysis of complaints and compliments.

All customer feedback needs to be acknowledged and comments incorporated in an action plan, perhaps a SIP. Review customer satisfaction measurements and analyse any variations to identify any actions that should be taken to address them.

4.5.8   Review and revise SLAs, service scope, OLAs, contracts, and any other underpinning agreements

All agreements and underpinning agreements must be reviewed periodically – at least annually – to ensure they remain current, comprehensive and aligned with business needs and strategy.

Ensure the services covered and the targets for each are still relevant.

Any changes need to be made under change management control.

Ensure that all targets in underpinning or 'back to back' agreements are aligned with, and support, targets agreed in the SLAs or OLAs. Where there are several layers of underpinning agreements ensure the targets at each layer are aligned with, and support, the targets at the higher levels.

4.5.9   Develop and document contacts and relationships

Develop trust and respect with the business, especially with the key business contacts.

Identify the stakeholders, customers and key business managers and service users.

Assist with maintaining accurate information within the service portfolio and service catalogue.

Ensure that the correct relationship processes are in place to achieve objectives and that they are subjected to continual improvement.

Conduct and complete customer surveys, assist with the analysis of the completed surveys and ensure that actions are taken on the results.

Act as an IT representative, organizing and attending user groups.

Facilitate the development and negotiation of appropriate, achievable and realistic SLRs and SLAs between the business and IT.

Ensure the business, customers and users understand their responsibilities and commitments to IT (i.e. IT dependencies).

4.5.10 Handling complaints and compliments

Develop, maintain and operate procedures for logging, acting on and resolving all complaints, and for logging and distributing compliments.

4.6   TRIGGERS, INPUTS, OUTPUTS AND INTERFACES (SD 4.3.6)

Triggers include:

- Changes in the strategy, policy or service portfolio, such as new or changed business requirements or new or changed services
- New or changed agreements, SLRs, SLAs, OLAs or contracts
- Service review meetings and actions and service breaches
- Periodic activities such as reviewing, reporting and customer satisfaction surveys, as well as compliments and complaints.

Inputs include:

- Business information from an organization's business strategy, plans and financial plans, and information on its current and future requirements
- Business impact analysis, providing information on the impact, priority, risk and number of users associated with each service
- Details of any agreed, new or changed business requirements
- Strategies, policies and constraints from service strategy, the service portfolio and service catalogue
- Customer and user feedback, complaints and compliments
- Other inputs include advice, information and input from any of the other processes (e.g. incident management, change management, capacity management and availability management), together with the configuration management

system (CMS), the existing SLAs, SLRs, OLAs and underpinning contracts (UCs), and past service reports on the quality of service delivered.

Outputs include:

- Service reports based on SLAs, OLAs and UCs
- Service improvement opportunities for inclusion in the CSI register
- Service quality plan, documenting and planning the overall improvement of service quality
- Document templates, format and content for SLAs, SLRs and OLAs, aligned with corporate standards
- SLAs, SLRs and OLAs
- Minutes and actions of service review meeting, and minutes of SLA and service scope review meeting
- Revised contracts to align with changes to SLAs or new SLRs.

Key interfaces are:

- **Business relationship management** Ensures that there is a full understanding of business needs and priorities and that there is customer involvement with the work of SLM
- **Service catalogue management** Provides accurate service information supporting the determination of the SLA framework and details of business and customer units that need to be engaged in the SLM process
- **Supplier management** Is involved with the negotiations when support is provided via external suppliers under contract. Manages performance of suppliers to ensure SLAs are met

- **Financial management for IT services** Validates the predicted costs of customer services delivered at the service levels required so that decisions can include comparisons of actual and predicted costs
- **Availability, capacity, IT service continuity and information management** All help to define service level targets.

4.7 INFORMATION MANAGEMENT (SD 4.3.7)

SLM provides key information on all operational services, their expected targets and the service achievements and breaches. It helps with management of the service catalogue and also provides information and trends on customer satisfaction, including complaints and compliments.

SLM is crucial in providing information on the quality of IT services provided to the customer, and information on the customer's expectation and perception of that quality of service. This information should be widely available to all areas of the service provider organization.

4.8 CRITICAL SUCCESS FACTORS AND KEY PERFORMANCE INDICATORS (SD 4.3.8)

The efficiency and effectiveness of the process can be measured by identifying critical success factors (CSFs) for the process, each CSF being supported by key performance indicators (KPIs):

- **CSF** Manage the overall quality of IT service needed, both in the number and level of services provided and managed:
  - **KPI** Percentage reduction in SLA targets missed and threatened

- **KPI** Percentage increase in customer perception and satisfaction of SLA achievements, via service reviews and customer satisfaction survey responses
- **KPI** Percentage reduction in SLA breaches because of third-party support contracts (UCs)
- **KPI** Percentage reduction in SLA breaches because internal OLAs are in place
- **CSF** Deliver the service as previously agreed at affordable costs:
  - **KPI** Total number and percentage increase in fully documented SLAs in place
  - **KPI** Percentage increase in SLAs agreed against operational services
  - **KPI** Percentage reduction in the costs associated with service provision
  - **KPI** Frequency of service review meetings
- **CSF** Manage the interface with the business and user:
  - **KPI** Percentage increase in services covered by SLAs
  - **KPI** Percentage increase in SLA reviews completed on time
  - **KPI** Percentage reduction in outstanding SLAs for annual renegotiation
  - **KPI** Percentage increase in the coverage of OLAs and third-party contracts in place, while possibly reducing the total number of agreements (through consolidation and centralization)
  - **KPI** Reduction in the number and severity of SLA breaches
  - **KPI** Effective review and follow up of all SLA, OLA and UC breaches.

4.9 CHALLENGES AND RISKS (SD 4.3.9)

Challenges include:

- Identifying suitable customer representatives with whom to negotiate
- Lack of SLM experience; using draft SLAs and engaging with the more enthusiastic customer groups helps mitigate the risk of failure
- Ensuring all the appropriate and relevant customer requirements, at all levels, are identified and incorporated in SLAs, including targets that are realistic, achievable and affordable
- Getting the SLAs agreed and signed
- Underpinning the SLAs with OLAs and supplier contracts
- Publishing and communicating the agreed service levels to all stakeholders, including the service desk
- Establishing monitoring of service performance.

Risks include:

- A lack of accurate input, involvement and commitment from the business and customers
- Lack of the required tools and resources to agree, document, monitor, report and review agreements and service levels and access to an up-to-date CMS and SKMS
- Process becomes bureaucratic and administrative rather than proactive and delivering measurable benefit to the business
- Business and customer measurements are too difficult to measure and improve, so they are not recorded
- Inappropriate and poor business and customer contacts, communications and relationships are developed
- Customer expectations are high while perceptions of the services delivered are low.

4.10   ROLES AND RESPONSIBILITIES (SD 6.3.7)

4.10.1 Service level management process owner

- Carrying out the generic process owner role for the SLM process (see section 1.5)
- Liaising with the business relationship management process owner to ensure that there is coordination and communication between the two processes
- Working with other process owners to ensure that an integrated approach is taken to the design and implementation of the service catalogue, service portfolio, business relationship and SLM.

4.10.2 Service level management process manager

- Carrying out the generic process manager role for the SLM process (see section 1.5)
- Ensuring the current and future service requirements of customers are identified, understood and documented in the SLA and SLR documents
- Negotiating and agreeing the levels of service to be delivered with the customer (either internal or external); formally documenting these levels of service in SLAs, with underpinning OLAs and agreements
- Ensuring service reports are produced for each customer service and that any SLA breaches are highlighted, investigated and actions taken to prevent recurrence
- Ensuring service performance reviews are scheduled, regularly carried out and documented, with actions agreed, including identified improvement initiatives that are progressed and reported

- Reviewing service scope, SLAs, OLAs and other agreements on a regular basis (ideally at least annually)
- Ensuring all changes are assessed for their impact on service levels, including SLAs, OLAs and UCs, including attendance at change advisory board meetings if appropriate
- Developing relationships and communication with stakeholders, customers and key users, including managing complaints
- Measuring, recording, analysing and improving customer satisfaction
- Other roles include service owner and business relationship manager roles within SLM.

5   Demand management

Demand management is a critical aspect of service management.

Poorly managed demand is a risk for service providers because demand can be uncertain. Excess capacity can generate cost without creating the perceived value that provides a basis for cost recovery. In reality, however, it creates value by delivering higher levels of service assurance. On the other hand, insufficient capacity can impact the quality of services and limit their growth.

Service management needs a tight coupling between demand and capacity. Ideally this should be synchronized, as unlike traditional products, which may be created in a production cycle and then stored to satisfy a later sales cycle demand, IT services may be used only at the point when they are required.

Service level agreements (SLAs), forecasting, planning, and coordination with the customer can reduce the uncertainty in demand but not eliminate it. Demand management techniques such as off-peak pricing, volume discounts and differentiated service levels can influence demand but do not drive or create it.

Demand forecasts and business patterns can be used to align the capacity available with a service. Some types of capacity can be quickly adjusted as required; they can either be increased to support demand or they can be released when not in use.

5.1   PURPOSE AND OBJECTIVES (SS 4.4.1)

The purpose of demand management is to understand, anticipate and influence customer demand for services ensuring that there is capacity to meet the demand. This involves working at every stage of the service lifecycle to ensure that services are designed, tested and delivered to achieve the business outcomes at the appropriate level of activity.

The objectives of demand management include:

- Identify and analyse the patterns of business activity (PBA) to understand the demand for the service, ensuring the design meets the demand and business outcomes
- Define and analyse user profiles (UPs) to understand service demand from different types of user
- Work with capacity management to ensure that adequate resources are available to meet service demand, while maintaining a balance between the cost of the service and the value it achieves
- Ensure that resources can meet fluctuating demand and manage situations where demand exceeds the capacity available.

5.2   SCOPE (SS 4.4.2)

Demand management focuses on the business and user aspects of providing services and does not include those areas of resourcing and technology that are undertaken by capacity management. However, the two processes do work closely together.

Activities of demand management include identifying and analysing the PBA associated with services, identifying UPs and service usage patterns, and working with capacity management to influence demand for services.

5.3   VALUE TO THE BUSINESS (SS 4.4.3)

Demand management enables executives to evaluate the investment required to achieve business outcomes. By understanding the interactions of services, resources and capabilities, a balance between the cost of the service and the value of the business outcome it supports can be achieved.

5.4 POLICIES, PRINCIPLES AND BASIC CONCEPTS (SS 4.4.4)

Strategically the main aim of demand management is to match supply to demand. Services are dynamic and demand for them is tightly coupled with the capacity needed to supply them. The cycle of demand and supply will only function effectively while service assets have available capacity.

To balance supply and demand, service assets need to be geared to meet the dynamic patterns of demand. This involves anticipating changes in demand by recognizing when demand is increasing or decreasing and defining a mechanism to scale either investment or supply as required.

The actions required to achieve this include service identification, quantifying PBA, specification of the appropriate architecture for demand, capacity and availability planning, and performance management tuning.

Demand activities are required throughout all stages of the service lifecycle:

- **Service strategy** Identify services, outcomes and associated PBA using utilization scenarios to forecast demand, and support service portfolio management (SPM)
- **Service design** Confirm the customer availability and performance requirements, validate the design of service assets and contribute to the sizing of service continuity options

- **Service transition** Test and validate services for forecast utilization and PBA
- **Service operation** Carry out performance tuning or corrective action if demand exceeds normal levels
- **Continual service improvement** Identify trends in PBA and initiate appropriate changes to the capabilities of the service provider or to the behaviour of the customers.

5.5 PROCESS ACTIVITIES, METHODS AND TECHNIQUES (SS 4.4.5)

5.5.1 Identify sources of demand and forecasting

Information required for forecasting the future demand for services comes from various sources, including business plans, marketing plans and forecasts, production plans, sales forecasts and details of new product launches.

5.5.2 Patterns of business activity

Customer assets (e.g. people, processes and applications) undertake business activities which are performed in patterns. PBA represent the dynamics of the business, including interactions with customers, suppliers, partners and other stakeholders. As PBA generate revenue, income and costs, they account for most business outcomes.

Each pattern of business activity identified is documented using a PBA profile which includes classification attributes (frequency, volume, location and duration), requirements (performance, security, privacy, latency and tolerance for delays) and service asset requirements. PBA can alter over time with changes and improvements in the business.

5.5.3 User profiles

UPs are based on roles and responsibilities within organizations. They can include processes and applications as well as staff, since processes may be automated and so consume services on their own. Therefore, both processes and applications can have UPs.

Each UP can be associated with one or more predefined PBA, allowing for aggregation and relationships between diverse PBA to be made. UPs represent patterns that are persistent and correlated, ensuring a systematic approach to understanding and managing demand from customers. Table 5.1 shows an example of UPs matched with PBA.

PBA and UPs provide the basis for managing demand for the service by:

■ Enabling customers to better understand their business activities and view those activities as consumers of services and producers of demand
■ Giving service providers the information they need to sort and serve demand with appropriately matched services, service levels and service assets.

Sources of demand with similar workload characteristics can be identified and classified into distinct segments. Service designs, models and assets can then be specialized to serve a specific type of demand more effectively and efficiently. This focus leads to optimized service assets that meet the needs of groups of users with similar requirements, which will lead to increased customer satisfaction.

PBA and UPs should be managed as part of normal change control procedures.

Table 5.1 User profiles matched with patterns of business activity (example)

User profile	Applicable pattern of business activity	PBA code
Senior executive (UP1)	Moderate travel – domestic and overseas; highly sensitive information; zero latency on service requests; high need for technical assistance; needs to be highly available to the business	45 21
Highly mobile executive (UP2)	Extensive travel – domestic and overseas; sensitive information; low latency on service requests; moderate need for technical assistance; high customer contact; needs to be highly available to customers	33 06 17
Office-based staff (UP3)	Office-based administrative staff; low travel – domestic; medium latency on service requests; low need for technical assistance; full-featured desktop needs; moderate customer contact; high volume of paperwork; needs to be highly productive during work hours	44 13 12

5.5.4 Activity-based demand management

Business processes are the primary source of demand for services. PBA influence service demand patterns, as illustrated in Figure 5.1. Therefore, customer business patterns need to be identified, analysed and codified to provide input to capacity management, and visualized in terms of demand for supporting services and underlying service assets.

Demand patterns can occur at multiple levels, so activity-based demand management can daisy-chain demand patterns to ensure business plans are synchronized with service management plans.

5.5.5 Develop differentiated offerings

Since different levels of performance are required at different times, demand management works with SPM to define service packages that meet the variations in PBA.

Figure 5.1 Business activity influences patterns of demand for services

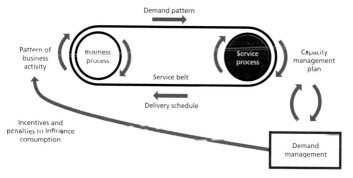

5.5.6   Management of operational demand

During service operation, demand management has to manage or influence demand in the case of over-utilization of services or resources. This situation can occur as a result of inaccurate PBA, changes to the business environment and inaccuracies in the service provider's forecasts. Demand management works with capacity management, service level management (SLM), SPM and financial management to influence demand.

5.6   TRIGGERS, INPUTS, OUTPUTS AND INTERFACES (SS 4.4.6)

Triggers include:

- Customer requests for new or changed services, or strategic initiatives via SPM
- Information on PBA or UPs required for definition of a service model
- Performance issues or potential SLA breaches due to utilization rates.

Inputs include:

- Initiatives to create a new service or change an existing service
- Service models for validation
- Customer, service and customer agreement portfolios containing information related to demand and supply
- Charging models and chargeable items
- Service improvement plans.

Outputs include:

- UPs and PBA (documented in service and customer portfolios)

- Policies for managing over- or under-utilization of resources and services
- Documentation of options for differentiated offerings used to create service packages.

Key interfaces include:

- **SPM** Information provided for the creation and evaluation of service models, identification of UPs and definition of service packages
- **Financial management for IT services** Provision of cost of demand based on forecast PBA and regulation of demand at times of over-utilization through differential charging
- **Business relationship management** Information regarding customers' business activities
- **SLM** Agreements that include the levels of customer utilization and the performance required
- **Capacity management** Works closely with demand management to achieve a balance of supply and demand, and provide operational monitoring of the service to determine trends in utilization
- **IT service continuity management and availability management** Use demand information to perform business impact analysis and to determine when service availability is most important.

5.7   INFORMATION MANAGEMENT (SS 4.4.7)

The main sources of information for demand management are the service, customer and project portfolios, together with minutes of meetings between business relationship management and the customer, SLAs and the configuration management system.

5.8   CRITICAL SUCCESS FACTORS AND KEY PERFORMANCE INDICATORS (SS 4.4.8)

The efficiency and effectiveness of the process can be measured by identifying critical success factors (CSFs) for the process, each CSF being supported by key performance indicators (KPIs):

- **CSF** The service provider has identified and analysed PBA and is able to use these to understand the levels of service demand:
  - **KPI** PBA are defined for each relevant service
  - **KPI** PBA are translated into workload information by capacity management
- **CSF** The service provider has defined and analysed UPs and is able to use these to understand typical demand for services from different user types:
  - **KPI** UPs are defined containing service demand profiles for that user type
- **CSF** A process exists whereby services are designed to meet the PBA and business outcomes:
  - **KPI** Demand management activities are routinely included as part of defining the service portfolio.

5.9   CHALLENGES AND RISKS (SS 4.4.9)

Challenges include:

- The availability of information about business activity
- It can be difficult for customers to break down activities in a way that is meaningful to the service provider
- A lack of SPM and service portfolio would make it difficult to find information on business requirements, value and priority of services.

Risks include:

- Inaccurate or missing configuration management data could affect impact assessments of changes in demand on the infrastructure
- SLM could be unable to determine and agree utilization levels, and this could cause imbalances between supply and demand for services

5.10   ROLES AND RESPONSIBILITIES (SS 6.8.10)

5.10.1 Demand management process owner

- Carrying out the generic process owner role for the demand management process (see section 1.5)
- Working with other process owners to ensure there is an integrated approach to the design and implementation of demand management.

5.10.2 Demand management process manager

- Carrying out the generic process manager role for the demand management process (see section 1.5)
- Identifying and analysing PBA to understand levels of service demand
- Defining and analysing UPs to understand demand from different user types
- Assisting in the design of services to meet PBA and business outcomes
- Maintaining a balance between the cost of service and the value it achieves by ensuring adequate resources and capacity are available

■ Gearing utilization of resources to meet fluctuating demand levels and anticipating, preventing or managing situations where demand exceeds capacity.

6 Supplier management

6.1 PURPOSE AND OBJECTIVES (SD 4.8.1)

The purpose of supplier management is to obtain value for money from suppliers and to provide a seamless quality of IT service to the business, ensuring that all contracts and agreements with suppliers support the needs of the business and meet its contractual obligations.

The primary objectives of supplier management are to:

- Obtain value for money from suppliers and contracts
- Ensure that contracts with suppliers are aligned with business needs, and support agreed targets in service level requirements (SLRs) and service level agreements (SLAs), in conjunction with SLM
- Manage relationships with suppliers
- Manage supplier performance
- Negotiate and agree contracts with suppliers and manage them through their lifecycle
- Maintain a supplier policy and a supporting supplier and contract management information system (SCMIS).

6.2 SCOPE (SD 4.8.2)

Supplier management includes the management of all suppliers and contracts needed to support the provision of IT services to the business. The process is adapted according to the importance of the supplier and/or contract and the potential business impact on the provision of services.

Supplier management includes:

- Implementation and enforcement of the supplier policy
- Maintenance of an SCMIS
- Supplier and contract categorization, evaluation, risk assessment and selection
- Development, negotiation and agreement of contracts
- Contract review, renewal, dispute resolution and termination
- Management of suppliers, sub-contracted suppliers and supplier performance
- Identification of improvement opportunities for inclusion in the CSI register and implementation of service and supplier improvement plans
- Maintenance of standard contracts, terms and conditions.

IT supplier management may have to comply with organizational or corporate standards, guidelines and requirements; for example, corporate legal, finance or purchasing.

Each supplier needs to be owned by a nominated person within the organization. A single individual may own the relationship for one or many suppliers.

6.3   VALUE TO THE BUSINESS (SD 4.8.3)

Supplier management provides value to the business by ensuring that:

- Suppliers and contracts provide value for money
- All targets in underpinning supplier contracts and agreements are aligned with business needs and agreed targets within SLAs
- End-to-end, seamless, high-quality IT services that are aligned with the business' expectation are delivered to the business.

Supplier management should align with corporate and all other IT and service management processes, particularly information security management (ISM) and IT service continuity management.

6.4   POLICIES, PRINCIPLES AND BASIC CONCEPTS (SD 4.8.4)

A supplier strategy and policy drives all supplier management activities. Policies document management directions that guide supplier-related decisions and ensure execution of the strategy. They include methods of communication, allocation of roles, ownership of data, and supplier standards and guidelines relating to contracts and agreements.

An SCMIS, with clearly defined supplier management roles and responsibilities, achieves consistency and effectiveness in the implementation of the policy. The SCMIS forms an integrated element of a comprehensive configuration management system (CMS) or service knowledge management system, containing a complete set of reference information for all supplier management procedures and activities.

6.5   PROCESS ACTIVITIES, METHODS AND TECHNIQUES (SD 4.8.5)

For external service providers, or suppliers, a formal contract with defined, agreed and documented responsibilities and targets needs to be established and managed, from the identification of the business need to the operation and cessation of the contract.

New supplier and contract requirements are defined as follows:

■ Produce a statement of requirements and/or invitation to tender

- Ensure conformance to strategy or policy
- Prepare the initial business case, including options (internal and external), costs, timescales, targets, benefits and risk assessment.

New suppliers and contracts are evaluated as follows:

- Determine the approach to sourcing; for example, single provider, multi-sourced or partnering (partnering relationships are characterized by strategic alignment, integration, information flow, openness, collective responsibility, and shared risk and reward)
- Establish the evaluation criteria; for example, the importance and impact of the service on the business, supplier capability (both personnel and organizational), quality, risks and cost
- Evaluate alternative supplier options and select supplier(s)
- Negotiate contracts, targets and the terms and conditions, including service description and standards, workload ranges, management information to be reported, responsibilities and dependencies
- Agree and award the contract: formal contracts are appropriate for external supplier agreements where an enforceable commitment is required. For internal service providers an underpinning agreement such as an operational level agreement (OLA) formalizes the arrangement via service level management (SLM).

Supplier and contract categorization and maintenance of the SCMIS are carried out as follows:

- Assess or reassess the supplier and contract; for example, based on the risk and impact of using a supplier against the value and importance of the supplied service to the business
- Categorize the supplier:

- Categorize suppliers as 'strategic', 'tactical', 'operational' or 'commodity' to ensure that appropriate levels of time and effort are spent managing the supplier relationship
- Categorization can be based on contract price, business value (contribution to the business value chain), or level of service customization (increasing business value but also dependencies, risk and cost)
- Business services may depend on a mix of internal and external suppliers of different categorizations. Supply chain analysis can be used to identify the mapping between business services and suppliers. Supply chain management can then ensure clarity of requirements for each supplier to ensure overall business service levels are achieved

■ Update the SCMIS, containing supplier details, service and product summaries, ordering details and contract details.

Establish new suppliers and contracts:

■ Set up the supplier service and contract, within the SCMIS and any other associated corporate systems via change management

■ Establish risk management activities for the supplier; for example, operational risk assessments and/or business impact analysis. This needs to be ongoing, reflecting changes to business needs, the contract or the operational environment

■ Undertake transition of new supplier and contract into operational service

■ Establish contacts, relationships and reviews, and add them to the SCMIS.

Manage supplier and contract performance:

- Nomination of a single individual who is accountable for all aspects of each supplier relationship
- Management and control of the operation and delivery of the service or products, including integrated processes and systems, and escalation
- Service and supplier performance reports and reviews – these should be more frequent and more extensive for the more important suppliers, and should include any improvement activities that are required or in progress
- Governance of the supplier, contracts and the relationship (communication, risks, changes, failures, improvements, contacts, interfaces)
- Control of major service improvements through service improvement plans (SIPs)
- Ongoing maintenance of the SCMIS
- Service, service scope and contract reviews, at least annually, considering overall performance, original and current business needs, delivery of value for money, business satisfaction and benefits realization.

Contract renewal and/or termination:

- Contract review to ensure that the contract continues to meet business needs. Consider aspects such as contract delivery and governance, relevance to future needs, changes required, performance and pricing against benchmarks or market assessments
- Assess the impact, risks, costs (including exit costs), legal implications and benefits for any proposed change of supplier
- Renegotiate and renew or terminate and/or transfer contract and service.

The business, IT, finance, purchasing and procurement need to work together to ensure that all stages of the contract lifecycle are managed effectively.

6.6   TRIGGERS, INPUTS, OUTPUTS AND INTERFACES (SD 4.8.6)

Triggers include:

■ New or changed business and IT strategies, policies or plans
■ New or changed business needs, services or requirements within agreements; for example, SLAs
■ Periodic activities such as reviewing, revising or reporting, including review and revision of supplier management policies, reports and plans
■ Requests from other areas, particularly SLM and security management, for assistance with supplier issues
■ Requirements for new contracts, contract renewal or contract termination
■ Recategorization of suppliers and/or contracts.

Key inputs include:

■ Business information, business strategy and plans, financial plans, and current and future requirements
■ Supplier and contracts strategy, sourcing policy and types of suppliers and contracts used
■ Supplier plans and strategies, supplier business plans and strategies, technology developments and plans, current financial status and projected business viability
■ Supplier contracts, agreements and targets, and performance information, including performance issues, incidents and problems relating to poor contract or supplier performance

- Financial information, including the cost of supplier services and supplier failure and the cost of contracts
- Service information, including details of services in the service portfolio and service catalogue, service level targets within SLAs and SLRs, and the actual service performance.

Outputs include:

- SCMIS: this holds the information needed by all sub-processes within supplier management
- Supplier and contract performance information and reports
- Supplier and contract review meeting minutes
- Supplier SIPs
- Supplier survey reports.

Key interfaces include:

- **IT service continuity management** Managing continuity service suppliers
- **SLM** Ensuring that targets, requirements and responsibilities support all SLR and SLA targets, and investigating any SLR or SLA breaches caused by poor supplier performance
- **ISM** Managing supplier access to services and systems, and their conformance to ISM policies and requirements
- **Financial management for IT services** Providing adequate funds for supplier management requirements and contracts, plus guidance on purchasing and procurement
- **Service portfolio management (SPM)** Ensuring that all supporting services are accurately reflected in the service portfolio.

6.7   INFORMATION MANAGEMENT (SD 4.8.7)

All the information needed by supplier management should be contained in the SCMIS. This includes information relating to suppliers, contracts, and the operation of supporting services provided by suppliers. Supporting service details and their relationships with other services and components should also be in the service portfolio and aligned with the CMS.

6.8   CRITICAL SUCCESS FACTORS AND KEY PERFORMANCE INDICATORS (SD 4.8.8)

The efficiency and effectiveness of the process can be measured by identifying critical success factors (CSFs) for the process, each CSF being supported by key performance indicators (KPIs):

- **CSF** The business is protected against poor supplier performance or disruption:
  - **KPI** Increase in the number of suppliers meeting contracted targets
  - **KPI** Reduction in the number of breaches of contracted targets
- **CSF** Supporting services and targets align with business needs and targets.
  - **KPI** Increase in the number of service and contractual reviews held with suppliers
  - **KPI** Increase in the number of supplier and contractual targets aligned with SLR and SLA targets
- **CSF** Availability of services is not compromised by supplier performance:
  - **KPI** Reduction in the number of service breaches caused by suppliers

- **KPI** Reduction in the number of potential service breaches caused by suppliers
- **CSF** There is ownership and awareness of supplier and contractual issues:
    - **KPI** Increase in the number of suppliers with nominated supplier managers
    - **KPI** Increase in the number of contracts with nominated contract managers.

6.9 CHALLENGES AND RISKS (SD 4.8.9)

Challenges include:

- Continually changing business and IT needs and managing significant change in parallel with delivering existing service
- Working with an imposed non-ideal contract; for example, with poor targets or terms and conditions
- Insufficient expertise retained within the organization, or personality conflicts
- Being tied into long-term contracts with no possibility of improvement, which have punitive penalty charges for early exit
- Supplier dependencies on the organization in fulfilling the service delivery (e.g. for a data feed) leading to accountability issues for poor service performance
- Disputes over charges
- Communication – not interacting often enough or quickly enough or not focusing on the right issues.

Major risks include:

- Lack of commitment from the business and senior management
- Legacy of badly written and agreed contracts that do not underpin or support business needs or SLR/SLA targets

- Suppliers agree to targets and service levels within contracts that are impossible to meet, or suppliers fail or are incapable of meeting the terms and conditions of the contract
- Supplier's personnel or organizational culture is not aligned with that of the service provider or the business
- Lack of clarity and integration by supplier with service providers' service management processes, policies and procedures
- Suppliers are not cooperative or willing to participate in the supplier management process
- Suppliers are taken over and relationships, personnel and contracts are changed
- Poor corporate financial processes, such as procurement and purchasing, that do not support good supplier management.

6.10   ROLES AND RESPONSIBILITIES (SD 6.3.12)

6.10.1 Supplier management process owner

- Carrying out the generic process owner role for the supplier management process (see section 1.5)
- Working with business and other processes (including SLM, and corporate vendor management) to ensure coordination, communication and an integrated approach to design and implementation.

6.10.2 Supplier management process manager

- Carrying out the generic process manager role for the supplier management process (see section 1.5)
- Supporting the development and review (at least annually) of SLAs, contracts and agreements for suppliers, ensuring they are aligned with the requirements of the business and delivering value for money

- Maintaining and reviewing an SCMIS
- Reviewing and carrying out a risk analysis of all suppliers and contracts on a regular basis
- Ensuring that all supporting services are scoped and documented and that interfaces and dependencies between suppliers, supporting services and supplier processes are agreed and documented
- Updating contracts or SLAs when required, ensuring that the change management process is followed
- Monitoring, reporting and regularly reviewing supplier performance against targets, identifying improvement actions as appropriate and ensuring these actions are implemented
- Ensuring changes are assessed for their impact on suppliers, supporting services and contracts and attending change advisory board meetings when appropriate
- Coordinating and supporting IT supplier and contract managers, ensuring that each supplier and contract has a nominated owner within the service provider organization.

7   Financial management for IT services

7.1   PURPOSE AND OBJECTIVES (SS 4.3.1)

Financial management enables an organization to manage and use its resources to meet its business objectives. More specifically, financial management for IT services (FMITS) manages the IT service provider's budgeting, accounting and charging requirements. It is also the process that is used to quantify the value that IT services contribute to the business.

The purpose of FMITS is to secure the appropriate level of funding to design, develop and deliver services that meet the strategy of the organization, while ensuring that the service provider does not commit to services that it is not able to provide. It helps identify the balance between the cost and quality of service whilst maintaining the balance of supply and demand.

Financial management is applicable to all three service provider types: internal service provider, shared service unit and external service provider.

The objectives of FMITS include:

- Provide frameworks to identify, manage and communicate the cost of providing services and, where appropriate, cost recovery from the customer
- Evaluate the financial impact of new or changed strategies on the service provider
- Secure funding to manage the provision of services
- Facilitate good stewardship of service and customer assets
- Manage and report service expenditure on behalf of stakeholders

- Execute the financial policies and practices in the provision of services
- Account for money spent on the creation, delivery and support of services
- Forecast current and future financial requirements.

7.2   SCOPE (SS 4.3.2)

FMITS is a specialized area that requires an understanding of the world of finance, business and also technology. It is often a separate function, reporting either to the chief information officer or the chief financial officer.

Financial policies and practices within IT must be consistent with those of the rest of the organization. FMITS encourages better communication and reporting between IT and other business units.

In organizations with internal service providers, financial management plays a translational role between corporate financial systems and service management. A service-oriented accounting function provides far greater detail and understanding regarding service provision and consumption.

7.3   VALUE TO THE BUSINESS (SS 4.3.3)

The business benefits from the operational visibility, insights and improved decision-making that are enabled by having good financial management and financial data.

IT service providers use financial management to support the development and execution of their service strategy, thereby achieving enhanced decision-making, speed of change, service portfolio management, financial compliance and control, operational control and value capture and creation.

Financial management generates meaningful critical performance data to steer service design and strategic, tactical and operational decisions.

Specific benefits to the business include:

- The business is conducted in a financially responsible manner, operates legally and thereby reduces the risk of penalties for non-compliance
- Budgeting is accurate and covers the cost of service
- Understanding the cost of IT to each business unit allows cost recovery and (for Type III service providers) provides the ability to maintain profitability
- Matching IT services to business results in appropriate and controllable spending models and more predictable profitability
- Sound business decisions can be made regarding the use of and investment in IT.

7.4   POLICIES, PRINCIPLES AND BASIC CONCEPTS (SS 4.3.4)

7.4.1   Enterprise financial management policies

The enterprise financial management policies provide a framework within which IT must work. Policies that impact an IT service provider include:

- The level of financial expenditure that needs to be tracked (e.g. cost per desktop device or the total cost of all desktops)

- Configuration items (CIs) to record as financial assets and their classification
- Depreciation of fixed assets
- Management of taxes (e.g. an IT service that is sold externally is reported differently from one only used internally)
- Reporting of costs, whether the cost of services is accounted for individually or as an overall cost which is allocated back to the business units
- How revenue is accounted for (and linked to IT services)
- Compliance with legislative or other regulatory requirements.

An important policy decision is whether IT should be a cost or profit centre:

- **Cost centre** A business unit or department to which costs are assigned, but that does not charge for the services provided
- **Profit centre** A business unit that charges for providing services.

Although IT executives may participate in deciding whether IT should be a cost or profit centre, this is ultimately determined by the organization's executives and is a part of the enterprise financial policy.

A Type III service provider is a profit centre, since it is a business in its own right. However, the different units within the company (HR, sales, marketing) may be seen as either cost or profit centres.

7.4.2 Funding

Funding is the sourcing and allocation of money for a specific purpose. Funding refers to the means whereby an IT service provider obtains financial resources that pay for the design, transition, operation and improvement of IT services. Funding can be external (from revenue received from selling services to external customers), or internal (from other business units within the same organization).

The funding of IT services is an important decision, and ultimately impacts the make-up of services in the service portfolio, the quality of services and the models used to design, transition, operate and improve those services. Funding is also dependent on whether IT is viewed as a cost or profit centre.

Funding models can be used to define how and when the IT service provider will be funded. These include:

- **Rolling plan funding** As one cycle completes, another cycle of funding is added, encouraging a constant cycle of funding
- **Trigger-based funding** When an identified critical trigger occurs it sets off planning for a particular event
- **Zero-based funding** There is sufficient funding only to cover the actual cost of the IT organization or service. The financial balance is brought back to zero until another funding cycle begins.

7.4.3 Financial management for IT services and value

To calculate the value of IT services it is necessary to have clearly defined and properly executed practices for FMITS. The service provider and customer must have appropriate financial models and practices in place since the calculation of value is a joint responsibility.

7.4.4 Service economics

Return on investment (ROI) is used, together with service portfolio management and FMITS, to build healthy service economics for the service provider's organization:

- ROI is a concept for quantifying the value of an investment
- Customer perception is subjective and intangible factors can make it difficult to quantify the value of service management
- While ROI can be helpful in indicating the success of a service or service management implementation, a number of factors must be taken into account when using ROI calculations. These include:
    - ROI is focused only on financial metrics; it does not indicate the full potential return
    - ROI calculations should include measures to indicate whether the service, or service management project, has moved the organization closer to achieving its strategy
    - ROI that is only based on cost savings for the service provider will not be perceived by the business as a return on its investment
    - ROI calculations that focus only on the short-term results will often yield negative figures.

A key challenge when trying to fund ITIL projects is identifying a specific business imperative that depends on service management. Three techniques to support this are:

- **Business case** A means to identify business imperatives that depend on service management
- **Pre-programme ROI** Techniques for quantitatively analysing an investment in service management
- **Post-programme ROI** Techniques for retrospectively analysing an investment in service management.

7.4.4.1   Business case

A business case is a decision support and planning tool. Its structure varies, but it should always include detailed analysis, typically financial, of the business impact or benefits. Business impact is linked to business objectives; for example, the reason for considering a service management initiative.

A typical business case structure includes:

- **Introduction** Presents the business objectives addressed by the service
- **Methods and assumptions** Defines the boundaries of the business case; for example, time period, organizational costs and benefits
- **Business impacts** Financial and non-financial business case results
- **Risks and contingencies** The probability that alternative results may emerge
- **Recommendations** Any specific actions that are recommended.

While most of a business case argument relies on cost analysis, for a service management initiative the considerations are not just financial. Non-financial business impacts also need to be linked to business objectives to show value (see Table 7.1).

Linking business impacts to business objectives delivers a more compelling business case and enables both financial and non-financial analysis to be carried out.

7.4.5   Compliance

Compliance is the ability to demonstrate that proper and consistent accounting methods are being used.

Table 7.1 Common business objectives

Operational	Financial	Strategic	Industry
Shorten development time	Improve return on assets	Establish or enhance strategic positioning	Increase market share
Increase productivity	Avoid costs	Introduce competitive products	Improve market position
Increase capacity	Increase discretionary spending as a percentage of budget	Improve professionalism of the organization	Increase repeat business
Increase reliability	Decrease non-discretionary spending	Improve customer satisfaction	Take market leadership
Minimize risks	Increase revenues	Provide better quality	Be recognized as a producer of reliable or high-quality products or services

Operational	Financial	Strategic	Industry
Improve resource utilization	Increase margins	Provide customized offerings	Be recognized as low-price leader
Improve efficiencies	Keep spending to within budget	Introduce new products or services	Be recognized as compliant with industry standards
Meet contractual obligations	Ensure that performance supports revenue generation	Deliver to meet objectives and obligations	Be recognized as a reliable provider
Reduce customer complaints	Reduce the cost of rework	Improve customer retention	Be recognized as a provider of quality goods and services

Areas covered include financial asset valuation, capitalization practices, revenue recognition, and access and security controls. Compliance is easily addressed if the proper practices are known and clearly documented as part of the enterprise financial policy.

Public demand for accurate and meaningful data relating to the value of a company's transactions and assets has put greater pressure on enterprise financial management. Recent regulatory and standard-related changes have been introduced that impact financial management. These include:

- Public frameworks and standards (COBIT, ISO/IEC 20000, *Management of Risk* (M_o_R®))
- Regulations (Basel II, Sarbanes–Oxley, industry-specific regulations).

7.5 PROCESS ACTIVITIES, METHODS AND TECHNIQUES (SS 4.3.5)

There are three main processes that underpin FMITS: accounting, budgeting and charging, as illustrated in Figure 7.1.

7.5.1 Accounting

Through accounting the service provider can:

- Track actual costs against budget
- Support the development of a sound investment strategy
- Provide cost targets for service performance and delivery
- Make decisions being aware of the cost implications, reducing risk
- Support the introduction of charging
- Review the financial consequences of previous strategic decisions.

7.5.1.1 Cost model

A cost model is a framework that is used to determine the cost of service provision and facilitates assessments of costs and impacts of the proposed changes to the services provided.

Figure 7.1 Major inputs, outputs and activities of financial management for IT services

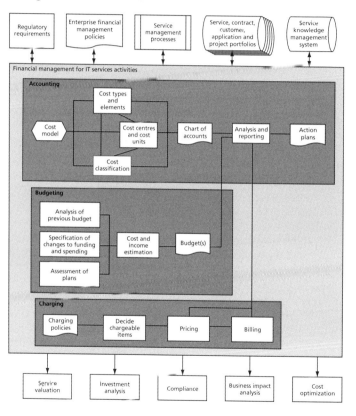

Cost models are used to:

■ Link expenditure to specific services
■ Support the development of a sound investment strategy
■ Enable fair division of shared service costs and form a basis for charging and pricing
■ Communicate the value of IT and enable the business to influence its IT investment.

Cost models used by IT service providers include cost by IT organization, cost by service, cost by customer, cost by location, and hybrid.

7.5.1.2   Cost centres and cost units

A cost centre is anything to which a cost can be allocated – for example, a service, location, department or business unit.

Cost centres have various uses, including: a basis for a charging policy; determining direct and indirect costs; providing categories for allocating and reporting costs; and assessing the impact of cost cutting or investment.

A cost unit is a category within a cost centre that enables a service provider to break down the high-level costs of the cost centre into more specific terms. This increases the accuracy of forecasting and the linking of costs to items that customers actually use.

7.5.1.3   Cost types and cost elements

There are at least two levels of category used to define costs, cost types and cost elements. Service providers should use categories that are appropriate for their specific situation and practices:

- **Cost types** These are the highest level of category to which costs are assigned in budgeting and accounting; for example, hardware, software, people, consulting services and facilities
- **Cost elements** These are the sub-categories of cost types, providing further breakdown to which costs are assigned in budgeting and accounting; for example, a cost type of 'people' with cost elements of payroll, staff benefits, expenses, training and overtime.

Cost elements in turn can be broken down into several hierarchies of sub-category. Some organizations may need two levels, others three or more.

7.5.1.4   Cost classification

The main classifications of costs are as follows:

- Capital or operational costs
  - **Capital** Cost of purchasing something that will become a financial asset. Fixed asset values are depreciated over multiple accounting periods
  - **Operational** Running costs of the IT services. Operational expenses are also known as current or revenue expenditure
- Direct or indirect costs
  - **Direct** Cost of providing an IT service that can be allocated in full to a specific customer, service, cost centre, project, etc.
  - **Indirect** Cost of providing an IT service that cannot be allocated in full to a specific cost centre; known as overheads, and allocated using a separate 'uplift' calculation
- Fixed or variable costs
  - **Fixed** Costs that do not vary with IT service usage; for example, server hardware

- **Variable** Costs that depend on how much an IT service is used, and cannot be fixed in advance
- Depreciation
  - A measure of the reduction in value of an asset over its life. It is predetermined by enterprise financial management policies. Common methods are straight-line, reducing balance and by usage.

7.5.1.5   Analysis, reporting and action plans

Income and expenditure are recorded in the chart of accounts (a list of all the accounts in use) which forms a basis for analysis and reporting. FMITS aligns the chart of accounts with its cost models, services and expenditure, avoiding duplications or independence from the enterprise chart.

The aims of analysis and reporting in FMITS include:

- Building an organization-wide understanding of the service provider's income, expenses and investments
- Communicating the cost of services to all stakeholders
- Providing a basis for controlling expenditure
- Ensuring funding of the service provider is adequate
- Ensuring each service is properly priced, competitive and the service provider is able to retain value for funding
- Helping customers calculate the value of services in terms of ROI
- Reviewing strategic decisions to ensure that the predicted financial outcomes were actually realized.

Analysis of the information can highlight issues that may require the initiation of action plans, such as deviation from the budget.

Close monitoring of financial reporting can indicate that a change has taken place and that action is required. The situation can be either unexpected, and require a quick response to deal with it, or anticipated, where the service provider already has a plan that can be adapted.

7.5.2   Budgeting

Budgeting is the activity of predicting and controlling the spending of money. Budgeting consists of a periodic negotiation cycle to set future budgets (usually annual) and the routine monitoring and adjusting of current budgets.

Budgeting is executed by all managers who have responsibility for any level of expenditure or income for their part of the organization. Each manager defines their plans, and the budgets that will enable execution of those plans.

Budget planning usually begins least one quarter before the current financial year end. Budgeting answers fundamental business questions, and then goes on to ensure that the answers are properly executed. Typical questions include:

- Does the organization have the resources needed to meet the objectives?
- Where will those resources come from?
- How many or how much of the resources will be needed and when?
- What commitment can be expected from every business unit to meet these objectives?
- Each month and quarter, where should the organization be in meeting its objectives?
- Where should costs be increased to keep up with performance that is better than expected?

■ Where should costs be cut if performance is worse than expected?

The budgeting process, policies and documents are defined and managed by enterprise financial management.

Budgeting activities include:

■ Analysis of previous budget
■ Assessment of plans within IT, which include: the organization's strategy; project plans; plans relating to customer environment changes; new services; technology updates; IT capacity and availability plans; service improvement plans; and services to be retired
■ Specification of changes to funding and spending
■ Cost and income estimation
■ Production of a budget documenting the items of expenditure, indicating when that expenditure is due to take place. Budgets typically consist of:
  – Expenses listed according to the categories in the chart of accounts, usually grouped by department
  – An indication of which service the item supports
  – Items for operational expenses and capital expense listed separately
  – Projects, listed separately with description and purpose
  – Expected income and sources of the income
  – Record of the planned income and expenditure, and the actual income and expenditure, for each month and quarter.

7.5.3   Charging

Charging is the activity whereby payment is required for services delivered. For internal service providers charging is optional and the IT service provider is treated as a cost centre, with charging referred to as 'chargeback', as it does not require a profit. Whether to charge for IT services is an important decision.

The arguments in favour of charging include:

- Charging places the customer in control of its IT spend
- Charging for services provides more accurate information, allowing more informed business decisions on the use of technology
- IT is able to operate with greater transparency and accountability
- Customers can compare the costs of the services with the business outcomes, increasing their appreciation of service value that is achieved
- Charging can encourage better or different use of IT services to support business outcomes at optimal cost
- Charging ensures that the financial implications of each request for a particular type or level of service are understood
- Charging can result in changes in behaviour; for example, ensuring that users use high-demand services at off-peak times.

The arguments against charging include:

- Charging can be a complex and bureaucratic process, involving expensive accounting tools
- Charging could change the politics of the organization negatively, especially if IT is the only department charging for its services

- Where financial reporting adequately represents the costs of providing services in business terms, there is less need for charging.

Introducing charging will fail unless the IT service organization has the support of the whole organization. It has to be simple, fair and realistic.

Decisions have to be made when charging is introduced. Typical areas that need to be determined are:

- **Charging policies** Determine how charging will work; this is defined by the office of the chief financial officer or financial controller. There are five decisions to be taken:
  - Whether to charge
  - Level of charges
  - How to influence customer behaviour when charging
  - How to handle customers who use another service provider at lower cost
  - How the level of service usage can be monitored
- **Level of cost recovery** Typical options are:
  - Cost recovery or break-even
  - Recovery plus additional margin IT recovers more than actual costs
  - Cross-subsidization, where some services are charged with an additional margin, which offsets the cost of other services
  - Notional charging, which is a type of financial reporting rather than charging; informing an internal customer of the cost of the service
- **Chargeable items** The lowest level at which a charge is measured, based on items that can be controlled by the customer (e.g. PCs). The customer can then manage its budget by controlling its demand for these items

- **Pricing** The activity for establishing how much customers will be charged. There are several options for deciding how much to charge, including:
  - **Cost price** As close as possible to the actual cost
  - **Cost plus price** Cost plus a percentage set by the organization or IT
  - **Going rate** Price comparable with that of similar service providers in similar organizations
  - **Market price** Price the same as that charged by external suppliers
  - **Fixed price** Price negotiated with the customer for a set period, based upon a predicted consumption
  - **Tiered subscription** Priced differently according to the service package option that has been selected
  - **Differential charging** Varying charges for different usages of the same services to reward some usage patterns over others
- **Billing** The production and presentation of invoices for services to a customer. There are three options:
  - **No billing** Invoices are not produced; costs are allocated by internal transfer
  - **Informational billing** Used with notional charging; invoices are produced but revenue is not collected
  - **Billing and collection** Invoices are produced and revenue is collected by the IT service provider from the customer.

7.6   TRIGGERS, INPUTS, OUTPUTS AND INTERFACES (SS 4.3.6)

Triggers include:

- Monthly, quarterly and annual reporting cycles, which form part of standard financial management

- Actions to accounting, budgeting or charging process that are required as a result of audits
- Financial information requests from other service management processes
- Investigation into new service opportunities
- Introduction of charging for IT services
- Financial information required for cost and impact assessment for RFC.

Inputs include:

- Regulatory requirements: financial management is subject to legislation and requirements from other statutory bodies
- Enterprise financial management policies, which form a basis for financial management for IT services
- Service management processes providing details of how money is spent and commitments to customers
- Information from service, contract, customer, application and project portfolios
- The service knowledge management system (SKMS) provides specific information about service assets and related investments.

Outputs include:

- Service valuation: the cost of the service relative to its business value
- Service investment analysis: the value of investment in a service can be determined using information and history provided by FMITS
- Compliance with financial regulation
- Business impact analysis: the effect on the business if the service is not available

■ Planning confidence: the level of confidence that service stakeholders have in the service provider being able to accurately forecast costs and returns.

Key interfaces include:

■ **Strategy management for IT services** FMITS is used to translate the organizational strategy into specific objectives for the service provider

■ **Service portfolio management (SPM)** Provides the service structure used to define cost models, accounting and budgeting systems and the basis for charging

■ **Business relationship management** Provides information on how the business measures the value of a service and what it is prepared to pay for services

■ **Capacity and availability management** Provides valuable information on technology options

■ **Change management and continual service improvement** Both use financial information as part of impact assessments and ROI of proposed improvements

■ **Service asset and configuration management** Provides basic information relating to assets and CIs

■ **All other service management processes** Use financial management to determine the costs and benefits of the process itself.

7.7   INFORMATION MANAGEMENT (SS 4.3.7)

The main sources required for information management include: financial management systems such as accounting, budgeting and charging; financial management policies; financial reporting structures; templates; spreadsheets; the organization's chart of accounts; and SKMS (of which financial management for IT services is an integral part).

7.8   CRITICAL SUCCESS FACTORS AND KEY PERFORMANCE INDICATORS (SS 4.3.8)

The efficiency and effectiveness of the process can be measured by identifying critical success factors (CSFs) for the process, each CSF being supported by key performance indicators (KPIs):

- **CSF** FMITS is a key component of evaluating strategies:
  - **KPI** All strategies have a comprehensive analysis of investment and returns based on information provided by FMITS
  - **KPI** A review of strategies indicates an accurate financial forecast within an acceptable percentage
  - **KPI** Timely and accurate provision of financial information for SPM analysis
- **CSF** Funding is available to support provision of the service:
  - **KPI** Internal service providers receive the required funding to deliver the agreed services and can break even at the end of the accounting period
  - **KPI** External service providers can sell services at the required levels of profitability
  - **KPI** Funding is available for research and development of new or improved services
- **CSF** The service provider must be able to account for the money spent on the creation, delivery and support of the services:
  - **KPI** The service provider uses an accounting system, configured to report costs by service

- **KPI** Regular reports are provided on the cost of services in design, transition and operation.

7.9   CHALLENGES AND RISKS (SS 4.3.9)

Challenges include:

- Financial reporting and cost models are not focused on the total cost of the service, leading to difficulties in demonstrating value to the customer
- Ensuring the chart of accounts and reporting is appropriate to the service provider as well as conforming to the enterprise standards
- Initially FMITS may find it difficult to locate financial data
- An organizational focus on cost-saving and cost-cutting, leading to reduced customer perception of service provider value
- Internal service providers experiencing difficulty in introducing charging
- External providers experiencing difficulty in pricing the services in such a way that there is a balance between the cost of delivery and value to the customer.

Risks include:

- Lack of a dedicated FMITS may result in poor investment decisions relating to services offered to the business
- Without FMITS organizations may find themselves more exposed to penalties for non-compliance with legislative or regulatory requirements
- Lack of staff with an understanding of both of IT service provision and cost accounting.

7.10   ROLES AND RESPONSIBILITIES (SS 6.8.9)

7.10.1 FMITS process owner

- Carrying out the generic process owner role for the financial management for IT process (see section 1.5)
- Working with other process owners to ensure an integrated approach to the design and implementation of FMITS.

7.10.2 FMITS process manager

- Carrying out the generic process manager role for the financial management for IT services process (see section 1.5)
- Compiling and formulating the annual IT budgets and submitting them for scrutiny and approval by the IT steering group
- Managing the IT budgets on a daily, monthly and annual basis; initiating corrective actions to balance income and expenditure in line with the budgets
- Producing regular statements of accounts for management information, thereby allowing managers to manage their own areas of the budgets
- Formulating and managing any recharging systems for IT customers
- Examining and reporting on value for money of all major activities, projects and proposed expenditure items within IT.

7.10.3 Budget holders

Various IT managers may be nominated as budget holders, to estimate, negotiate, agree, manage and report on the budgets for their own particular areas.

8 Business relationship management

8.1 PURPOSE AND OBJECTIVES (SS 4.5.1)

The purpose of business relationship management is twofold:

- To establish and maintain a business relationship between the service provider and the customer, based on an understanding of customer and business needs
- To ensure that the customer's expectations do not exceed its ability to pay and the service provider is able to meet these expectations before agreement is made.

The objectives of business relationship management include:

- Ensure that service providers understand the customer perspective and business drivers of the services
- Identify and determine the impact of any changes to the customer environment and technology on services
- Establish and articulate the business requirements for services
- Ensure that service providers meet the business needs of the customer and deliver value
- Provide a formal complaints process and escalation procedure for customers.

8.2 SCOPE (SS 4.5.2)

The scope can vary depending on whether the service provider is internal or external; for example:

- **Internal** Concerned with aligning the business objectives with the activity of the service provider
- **External** Concerned with maximizing the contract value through customer satisfaction.

The focus of business relationship management is to meet customer requirements by delivering appropriate services. This is achieved by understanding and communicating:

- The business outcomes that the customer wants to achieve
- The current service offerings to the customer; their use, agreed levels of service, quality, anticipated changes, how they can be optimized for the future and the potential impact of technology changes
- The levels of customer satisfaction and any plans required to mitigate the causes of dissatisfaction.

Although the activities of both business relationship management and service level management (SLM) involve customer interface there is a distinct difference between the processes. The focus of business relationship management is building customer relationships and defining customer requirements, whereas SLM is about defining and coordinating the tactical levels of performance of specific services.

8.3   VALUE TO THE BUSINESS (SS 4.5.3)

Business relationship management creates a forum for structured communication with customers, which leads to the achievement of current business outcomes and better alignment and integration of services in the future.

By promoting increased communication, business relationship management enables the service provider to understand the customer's needs and the customer is aware of the service provider's capabilities and services. Business relationship management acts as an arbiter, so that disagreements are resolved more quickly, and higher levels of trust are promoted between the two parties.

The focus on customer satisfaction promotes better understanding of whether the business objectives have been met and the associated value this brings.

8.4   POLICIES, PRINCIPLES AND BASIC CONCEPTS (SS 4.5.4)

8.4.1   Business relationship management and the business relationship manager

The role that a business relationship manager (BRM) undertakes often includes activities from other processes (e.g. project management, SLM) as they form the initial communication link between the service provider and customer. However, these actual activities are not part of the business relationship management process.

8.4.2   Customer portfolio

Business relationship management defines the customer portfolio where details of customers receiving services are maintained, enabling the service provider to quantify its commitments, investments and risk.

8.4.3   Customer agreement portfolio

Although the customer agreement portfolio is defined and maintained by SLM it is an important tool used by business relationship management.

8.4.4   Customer satisfaction

A key responsibility for business relationship management is to ensure that the customers are satisfied with the services they receive. Customer satisfaction measures can be used by business relationship management to compare them with the service provider performance, customer satisfaction targets and previous scores. A regular customer satisfaction survey (more comprehensive than service desk surveys) to assess whether the service achieves its objectives is undertaken throughout the service lifecycle.

Any differences between customers and users in the level of satisfaction reported are because the two groups consider the service from different perspectives (e.g. customers are concerned with the price of a service, whereas users are more interested in how well it performs). Business relationship management must therefore ensure that any trade-offs agreed with customers are properly communicated to all groups involved.

8.4.5 Service requirements

Defining and clarifying requirements is an essential part of business relationship management as customers find it difficult to articulate their requirements in a way that enables the service provider to design and build the service.

Customers sometimes define the solution, specifications, need or benefits rather than the actual requirement. Business relationship management investigates the business need, or opportunity validating it, creating the business case and determining the utility and warranty required.

8.4.6 Facilitator of strategic partnerships

Business relationship management facilitates when service providers need to be included in strategic discussions relating to the customer's business, ensuring that the correct people are involved, and that any relevant information is fed back to the appropriate processes.

8.5 PROCESS ACTIVITIES, METHODS AND TECHNIQUES (SS 4.5.5)

Business relationship management has activities relating to every stage of the service lifecycle, forming a bridge between the customer and the service provider as illustrated in Figure 8.1. The two main activities are:

- Representing the service provider to its customers
- Working with service portfolio management (SPM) and design coordination to ensure the service provider responds appropriately to the customer's requirements.

Business relationship management is rarely an end-to-end process as it is initiated to respond to specific situations either by the service provider or customer. A register is used to effectively manage requests, opportunities, complaints and compliments.

8.5.1 Initiation by the customer

Business relationship management is used by the customer to communicate to the service provider its needs, opportunities and requirements in a formal, organized manner. This avoids duplication if similar requests come from more than one customer and ensures that the request is directed to the correct service provider for assessment of a viable solution. The customer is provided with a single point of contact for all requirements and regular feedback on progress.

There are many ways in which business relationship management helps the customer, including:

- Defining opportunities either from a request for help or raised during regular review meetings

Figure 8.1 Business relationship management activities

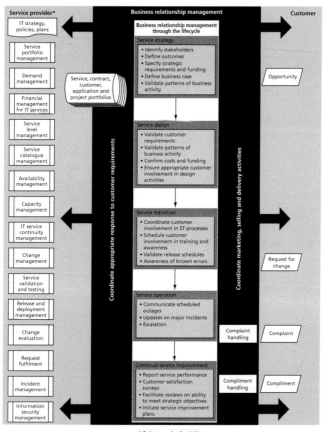

* Only a sample of activities
and processes are illustrated

■ Completing and submitting requests for change (RFC) and
   the appropriate documentation
■ Exploiting new opportunities or technology
■ Handling complaints:
   - **Relating to specific incidents** Although operational issues
     are handled through incident management, business
     relationship management is involved in major incidents,
     repeating incidents, new service incidents, incidents
     where there is a lack of progress information, and
     prioritization issues
   - **Not relating to specific incidents** Complaint handling
     procedures are needed to record and manage complaints.
     All outstanding complaints are regularly reviewed and
     analysed to identify any emerging trends, and where
     necessary initiating service improvement activities in
     conjunction with SLM and CSI
■ Handling compliments or unsolicited positive feedback
   relating to the quality of service. These are valuable and can
   be used to encourage staff. However, they should be
   analysed to ensure that the customer expectations or levels
   of service provided have not exceeded what is agreed, and
   consequently increased costs and the future expectations of
   the customer.

8.5.2 Initiation by service provider

Business relationship management can be used when the service
provider needs to engage with the customer, to discuss the
business implications of a new or changed service, or when extra
information is required on any future patterns of business
activity (PBA).

8.5.3 Business relationship management process through the lifecycle

Business relationship management is required at various stages through the service lifecycle but the involvement may differ from service to service. Areas of involvement for the BRM include:

Service strategy

- **IT strategy policies and plans** Agrees on the organizational scope and direction and enables identification of parameters for new and approved opportunities
- **SPM** Allows the identification of combinations of lines of service and service packages to meet business outcomes
- **Demand management** Identifies PBA and influencing factors
- **Financial management for IT services** Validates cost models and provides forecast information.

Service design

- **Project management** Confirms and clarifies the customer's requirements; then communicates, selects and schedules the appropriate customer resources
- **Financial management for IT services** Gains acceptance from the customer for changes in cost or modification of requirements during the design stage
- **SLM** Facilitates communication between the customer and service provider on changes to service levels and new requirements
- **Demand management** Assists in the definition, refinement and confirmation of PBA and accepts or rejects subsequent changes
- **Service catalogue management** The service descriptions in the service catalogue and service request catalogue are defined in conjunction with the customers

- **Availability management** Defines the customer's requirements for service availability and measurements
- **Capacity management** Ascertains customer transaction performance requirements
- **IT service continuity management** Facilitates customer identification of business impacts and recovery objectives.

Service transition

- **Change management** Raises RFCs, ensures customer representation and helps with impact assessment and scheduling of changes
- **Knowledge management** Ensures that customer 'knowledge needs' are captured in the knowledge management plans and customer information available in the service knowledge management system (SKMS)
- **Service testing and validation** Customer requirements are tested and customer resources to undertake testing are allocated
- **Release and deployment management** Participates in scheduling deployments and confirms that customers are adequately trained; it is therefore a key communication link.

Service operation

- **Request fulfilment** Helps the customer to use the service requests procedure or acts as a point of contact for key customers
- **Incident management** Supports the customer by getting involved in major incidents and escalations.

Continual service improvement

- **SLM** Schedules and conducts service reviews and monitors agreed actions

- **Seven-step improvement process** Identifies and communicates proposed improvements
- **Service reporting** Identifies requirements and uses reports to: influence customer perception; determine what monitoring is required; provide details for business reviews.

8.6   TRIGGERS, INPUTS, OUTPUTS AND INTERFACES (SS 4.5.6)

Triggers include:

- Initiation of a new service or changes to existing services
- Strategic initiatives or identification of new opportunities
- Services that have been chartered by SPM
- Customer requests, suggestions or complaints
- Scheduled customer meetings and customer satisfaction surveys.

Inputs include:

- Customer requirements, requests, complaints, escalations and compliments
- Service and customer strategies
- Service and project portfolios
- RFCs, SLAs and PBA.

Outputs include:

- Stakeholder definitions
- Defined business outcomes
- Agreement to fund (internal) or pay for (external) services
- Customer portfolio
- Service requirements for strategy, design and transition
- Customer satisfaction surveys, including results

- Schedules of customer activity in various service management process activities
- Schedule of training and awareness events
- Reports on customers' perceptions of service performance.

Interfaces include:

- **Strategy management for IT services** Identifies market spaces and is instrumental in development of strategic requirements
- **SPM** Identifies the requirements, creates service models and assesses and communicates the proposed services
- **FMITS** Provides information relating to customers' financial objectives and assists with return on investment (ROI) calculations and the introduction of charging
- **Demand management** Identifies user profiles, changes in business priorities and communicates and agrees the required demand management activities with the customer
- **Design processes including SLM, service catalogue, capacity, availability and IT service continuity management** Provides a bridge between the service provider and the customer for gathering and reporting of information
- **Change management and release and deployment** Assists with prioritization and impact assessments relating to changes and their release and deployment, thereby ensuring the appropriate levels of customer involvement
- **Continual service improvement** Identifies, validates and prioritizes improvements in conjunction with SLM.

8.7   INFORMATION MANAGEMENT (SS 4.5.7)

The main sources of information and documentation required by business relationship management include portfolios (service project, application, customer and customer agreement), and information gathered as a result of customer satisfaction surveys. The service catalogue is also used to communicate the quality and performance of services and requirements for changes to existing services.

8.8   CRITICAL SUCCESS FACTORS AND KEY PERFORMANCE INDICATORS (SS 4.5.8)

The efficiency and effectiveness of the process can be measured by identifying critical success factors (CSFs) for the process, each CSF being supported by key performance indicators (KPIs):

- **CSF** Ability to document and understand the customer's requirements of services, and associated business outcomes
  - **KPI** Customer requirements and business outcomes are documented and signed off by the customer (input to SPM and design)
- **CSF** Ability to measure customer satisfaction levels and knowing how to action the results
  - **KPI** Customer satisfaction levels are consistently high and are used as feedback to SPM and strategy management for IT services. Investigation of the causes and corrective actions are taken whenever scores are lower than the defined level
- **CSF** Ability to identify any changes to the customer environment that impact on the type, level or utilization of services provided

- **KPI** Customer satisfaction and retention rates are consistently high
- **KPI** Business relationship management provides input about changes to the customer environment that ultimately lead to improved customer satisfaction scores
- **CSF** Business relationship management must be able to measure whether the service provider is meeting the business needs of the customer
  - **KPI** The service provider is consistently rated above the minimum level in customer satisfaction surveys
  - **KPI** Service performance matches the business outcomes and is reported to the customer. Any deviations from expected achievements are documented and logged as an improvement opportunity on the CSI register
- **CSF** Formal complaints and escalation processes are available to customers
  - **KPI** The number of complaints and escalations is measured and trended over time by customer.

8.9 CHALLENGES AND RISKS (SS 4.5.9)

Challenges include:

- Promoting the use of business relationship management beyond the customer-friendly image that relates only to measuring levels of customer satisfaction
- A lack of credibility because of poor past service performance may affect the willingness of the customer to share the information required for the success of the process
- Confusion between the extended role of a business relationship manager and the scope of the business relationship management process.

Risks include:

- Confusion relating to the boundaries of business relationship management and other processes may lead to duplication of or missing activities
- A disconnect between customer-facing processes and technical processes may mean the service provider may become ineffectual.

8.10   ROLES AND RESPONSIBILITIES (SS 6.8.8)

The role of business relationship manager may also include those of process owner and process manager. There may be a number of business relationship managers, each focused on different customer segments or groups. The work may also entail additional activities as well as those directly relating to business relationship management.

8.10.1 Business relationship management process owner

- Carrying out the generic process owner role for the business relationship management process (see section 1.5)
- Ensuring interaction with other process owners to provide an integrated approach to the design and implementation of business relationship management.

8.10.2 Business relationship management process manager:

- Carrying out the generic process manager role for the business relationship management process (see section 1.5)
- Identifying customers' needs and ensuring that these can be met by providing an appropriate catalogue of services

- Ensuring that customer expectations do not exceed what they are willing to pay for and that the service provider is able to meet the expectations before agreement is reached
- Ensuring high levels of customer satisfaction
- Establishing and maintaining a constructive relationship between the service provider and customer
- Identifying any changes in customer environment and technology trends
- Establishing and articulating the business requirements for new or changed services
- Mediating whenever there are cases of conflicting requirements for services from different business units.

9 Technology and implementation

9.1 GENERIC REQUIREMENTS FOR IT SERVICE MANAGEMENT TECHNOLOGY (SD 7.1)

There are many tools and techniques that can be used to help with the design of services. They enable the following:

- Hardware design
- Software design
- Environmental design
- Process design
- Data design.

The tools and techniques are useful in:

- Speeding up the design process
- Ensuring standards are followed
- Prototyping, modelling and simulation
- Enabling 'What if?' analysis
- Enabling interfaces and dependencies to be checked
- Validating designs before development starts.

Developing service designs can be simplified by the use of tools that provide graphical views of the service and its constituent components. They can also be linked to auto-discovery tools to make the capture and maintenance of the relationships between all of the service components more efficient and accurate.

There is an opportunity to extend the use of these tools into day-to-day operation and, by linking to financial information, metrics and key performance indicators, they can be used to monitor and manage the service through all stages of its lifecycle.

The following generic activities are required to implement such an approach:

- Establish the generic lifecycle for IT assets (requirements, design and develop, build, test, deploy, operate and optimize, dispose) and define the principal processes, policies, activities and technologies within each stage of the lifecycle for each type of asset
- Formalize the relationships between different types of IT asset, and the relationships between IT asset acquisition and management and other IT disciplines
- Define all roles and responsibilities involved in IT asset activities
- Establish measures for understanding the (total) cost of ownership of an IT service
- Establish policies for the re-use of IT assets across services (e.g. at the corporate level)
- Define a strategy for the acquisition and management of IT assets, including how it should be aligned with other IT and business strategies.

9.2   EVALUATION CRITERIA FOR TECHNOLOGY AND TOOLS (SD 7.2)

Some generic points that organizations should consider when selecting any service management tool include:

- Data handling, integration, import, export and conversion
- Data backup, control and security
- Ability to integrate multi-vendor components, existing and into the future
- Conformity with international open standards
- Usability, scalability and flexibility of implementation and usage

- Support options provided by the vendor, and credibility of the vendor and tool
- The platform the tool will run on and how this fits the IT strategy
- Training and other requirements for customizing, deploying and using the tool
- Costs: initial and ongoing.

It is generally best to select a fully integrated tool, but this must support the processes used by the organization, and extensive tool customization should be avoided.

Consideration should also be given to the organization's exact requirements. These should be documented in a statement of requirements. Tool requirements should be categorized using MoSCoW analysis:

- **M** – MUST have this
- **S** – SHOULD have this if at all possible
- **C** – COULD have this if it does not affect anything else
- **W** – WON'T have this, but WOULD like in the future.

Each proposed tool can be evaluated against these criteria to ensure that the most appropriate option is selected.

9.3   PRACTICES FOR PROCESS IMPLEMENTATION

9.3.1   Service level requirements (SD 8.2)

As part of service level management, the service level requirements (SLRs) for all services will be ascertained and the ability to deliver against these requirements will be assessed. Finally the SLRs will be agreed in a formal service level agreement (SLA). For new services, the requirements must be ascertained at the start of the development process, not after completion. Building the service with SLRs uppermost in mind is essential from a service design perspective.

9.3.2 Risks to the services and processes (SD 8.3)

When implementing service design and IT service management (ITSM) processes, business as-usual practices must not be adversely affected. This aspect must be considered during the production and selection of the preferred solution to ensure that disruption to operational services is minimized. This assessment of risk should then be considered in detail in the service transition activities as part of the implementation process.

9.3.3 Implementing service design (SD 8.4)

The process, policy and architecture for the design of IT services will need to be documented and utilized to ensure that appropriate innovative IT services can be designed and implemented to meet current and future agreed business requirements.

What is ultimately required is a single, integrated set of processes, providing management and control of IT services throughout their entire lifecycle.

Areas of greatest need should be addressed first. A detailed assessment needs to be undertaken to ascertain the strengths and weaknesses of IT service provision.

It may be that 'quick wins' need to be implemented in the short term to improve the current situation. However, it is important that these are not at the expense of the long-term objectives.

Implementation priorities should be set against the goals of a service improvement plan (SIP). For example, if availability of IT services is a critical issue, focus on those processes aimed at maximizing availability (such as incident management, problem management, change management and availability management).

Establish a formal process and method for implementation and improvement of service design, with the appropriate governance in place. This formal process should be based on the six-stage continual service improvement model, as shown in Figure 9.1:

- **Step 1** Understand the vision by ascertaining the high-level business objectives. The 'vision-setting' should set and align business and IT strategies.
- **Step 2** Assess the current situation to identify strengths that can be built on and weaknesses that need to be addressed. Perform an analysis of the current position in terms of the business, organization, people and process.
- **Step 3** Develop the principles defined in the vision-setting and agree the priorities for improvement.
- **Step 4** Detail the SIP to achieve higher-quality service provision.
- **Step 5** Put in place measurements and metrics to show that the milestones have been achieved and that the business objectives and business priorities have been met.
- **Step 6** Ensure that the momentum for quality improvement is maintained.

The following are key elements for successful alignment of IT with business objectives:

- Vision and leadership in setting and maintaining strategic direction, clear goals, and measurement of goal realization in terms of strategic direction

Figure 9.1 The continual service improvement model

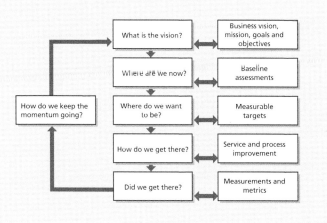

- Acceptance of innovation and new ways of working
- A thorough understanding of the business, its stakeholders and its environment
- IT staff understanding the needs of the business
- The business understanding the potential of IT
- Information and communication available and accessible to everyone who needs them
- Separately allocated time for people to become familiar with the material
- Continuous tracking of technologies to identify opportunities for the business.

9.4   CHALLENGES, CRITICAL SUCCESS FACTORS AND RISKS

9.4.1   Challenges

9.4.1.1   Service design (SD 9.1–9.2)

Challenges for service design include:

- Dealing with unclear or changing requirements from the business
- Clarifying business requirements and targets for services
- Poor relationships, communications or lack of cooperation between the IT service provider and the business
- Lack of information, monitoring and measurements
- Unreasonable targets and timescales previously agreed in SLAs and OLAs
- Poor supplier management and/or poor supplier performance
- Cost and budgetary constraints
- Determining ROI and the realization of business benefit.

9.4.1.2   Service transition (ST 9.1–9.3)

Challenges for service transition include:

- Managing contacts, interfaces and relationships across a large customer and stakeholder group
- Lack of harmonization and integration of the supporting processes and disciplines; for example, finance, engineering and human resources
- Developing standard performance measures and measurement methods across projects and suppliers
- Ensuring that the quality of delivery and support matches the business use of new technology

- Creating an environment that fosters standardization, simplification and knowledge-sharing
- Being able to assess, understand the balance and manage risk to IT and risk to the business.

9.4.1.3   Service operation (SO 9.1–9.3)

Challenges for service operation include:

- Lack of engagement with development and project staff
- Justifying funding on what are often seen as infrastructure costs
- Ensuring that the potential impact across all operational services is taken into account in each individual service design and transition
- Ensuring that a realistic assessment of true ongoing running costs, after transition, is taken into account in service design
- Ensuring service transition is effective in managing the transition from design to operation
- Understanding what and how to measure to demonstrate good performance
- Being increasingly involved in virtual or matrix teams can lead to confusion over who is accountable for ensuring specific activities are carried out.

9.4.2   Critical success factors

9.4.2.1   Service design

CSFs for service design include:

- Understanding business requirements and priorities and that they are taken into account when designing processes and services
- Ensuring good, ongoing communications with the affected individuals
- Involving as many people as possible in the design

■ Gaining commitment from senior management as well as from all levels of staff.

9.4.2.2 Service transition

CSFs for service transition include:

■ Understanding the different stakeholder perspectives that underpin effective risk management and maintaining commitment
■ Maintaining contact and managing all relationships
■ Integrating with other lifecycle stages, processes and disciplines that impact service transition
■ Maintaining new and updated knowledge in a format that can be found and used
■ Building a thorough understanding of risks that have impacted or may impact successful service transition of services in the service portfolio.

9.4.2.3 Service operation

CSFs for service operation include:

■ Ensuring senior management support; this is critical for maintaining the required funding and resources, as is visible support when new initiatives are launched
■ Ensuring business units understand the role they play in adhering to policies, processes and procedures – such as using the service desk to log all requests
■ Training service management staff to an appropriate level of understanding of the business, processes and tools
■ Ensuring the suitability of and ongoing funding for tools

- Clearly defining how things will be measured and reported – to provide staff with targets to aim for and to allow IT and business managers to review progress and identify opportunities for improvement.

9.4.3 Risks

Many risks are simply the opposite of CSFs, but the ultimate risk to the business is the loss of critical IT services, with its subsequent adverse impact on employees, customers and finances.

9.4.3.1 Service design

Risks to service design include:

- If any of the CSFs are not met, service design will not be successful
- Business requirements are not clear to IT staff
- An incorrect balance is struck between innovation, risk and cost while seeking a competitive edge, where desired by the business
- Business timescales do not allow sufficient time for proper service design
- The fit between infrastructure, customers and partners is not sufficient to meet overall business requirements
- A coordinated interface is not available between IT planners and business planners
- Policies and strategies are not available or are not clearly understood
- Insufficient resources and budget are available for service design activities.

9.4.3.2 Service transition

Risks to service transition include:

- Changes in accountabilities, responsibilities and practices of existing projects that demotivate the workforce
- Alienation of some key support and operations staff
- Additional, unplanned costs to services in transition
- Resistance to change and circumvention of the processes due to perceived bureaucracy
- Poor integration between processes causing process isolation and a 'silo' approach to delivering ITSM
- Loss of productive hours, higher costs, loss of revenue or perhaps even business failure as a result of poor service transition processes.

9.4.3.3 Service operation

Risks to service operation include:

- The ultimate risk to the business is the loss of critical IT services, with a subsequent adverse impact on employees, customers and finances
- If the initial design is faulty, a successful implementation will never give the required results, and redesign will ultimately be necessary
- Inadequate funding and resources available to maintain the infrastructure in a condition to guarantee ongoing service delivery
- Loss of momentum in the implementation of service management caused by day-to-day operational tasks taking priority
- Resistance to change caused by a reluctance to take new things on board

- Service management being viewed with suspicion by either IT or business
- Differing customer expectations.

9.5   PLANNING AND IMPLEMENTING SERVICE MANAGEMENT TECHNOLOGIES (SO 8.5)

There are a number of factors to consider when deploying and implementing ITSM support tools:

- **Licences** The cost of service management tools is usually determined by the type and number of user licences needed. Most tools are modular, so the specific selection of modules also affects the price. It is important to plan the provision of licences to avoid unexpected costs. There are a number of different licence types:
  - **Dedicated licences** For staff who need frequent and prolonged use of the module (e.g. service desk staff)
  - **Shared licences** For staff who use the module regularly, but with significant times when it is not needed. The ratio of licences to users should be calculated to give sufficient use at acceptable cost
  - **Web licences** For staff who need occasional access, or remote access, or who only need limited functionality
  - **Service on demand** The charge is based on the number of hours the service is used. This is suitable for smaller organizations or very specialized tools that are not used often. It can also include tools licensed as part of a consulting exercise (e.g. for carrying out capacity modelling)
- **Deployment** Many tools, especially discovery and event-monitoring tools, require deployment of clients or agents. This requires careful scheduling, planning and execution and should be subject to formal release and deployment

management. Devices may need to be rebooted and this should be planned. Change management should be used and the CMS updated. Particular care should be taken when planning deployment to laptops and other portable equipment that may not be connected all the time

- **Capacity checks** It may be necessary to check for sufficient system resources (e.g. disk space, CPU, memory) when planning a deployment. Allow sufficient lead time for upgrading or replacing equipment, and check network capacity

- **Timing of technology deployment** If tools are deployed too early, they can be seen as 'the solution' and essential process improvements may not be carried out. If tools are deployed too late, it can be hard to implement the new process. People need to be trained in use of the tool as well as the new or updated process, and timing for this must be planned, possibly with additional training after the tools have gone live

- **Type of introduction** The new tool often replaces an existing tool, and careful planning is needed for the transition. A phased approach can be more appropriate than a 'big bang' approach, but this depends on the exact circumstances. The key factor is planning what data needs to be migrated, and how. If data is being migrated, a data quality audit should be performed. An alternative approach is parallel running, in which case the old tool should run in a 'read only' mode to prevent mistakes.

10 Qualifications

10.1 OVERVIEW

The ITIL qualification scheme has four levels:

■ Foundation level
■ Intermediate level (Lifecycle and Capability streams)
■ ITIL Expert
■ ITIL Master.

There are also further complementary service management qualifications available that can contribute (accumulating credits) towards achievement of the ITIL Expert. Further information on the ITIL qualification scheme can be found at:

www.axelos.com

10.2 FOUNDATION LEVEL

The Foundation level ensures candidates gain knowledge of the ITIL terminology, structure and basic concepts, and comprehend the core principles of ITIL practices for service management. Foundation represents two credits towards the ITIL Expert.

10.3 INTERMEDIATE LEVEL

There are two streams in the Intermediate level, assessing an individual's ability to analyse and apply concepts of ITIL:

■ Lifecycle stream
■ Capability stream.

10.3.1 Lifecycle stream

The Lifecycle stream is built around the five core publications and is for candidates wanting to gain knowledge within the service lifecycle context. Each module achieves three credits.

10.3.2 Capability stream

The Capability stream is built around four practitioner-based clusters and is for candidates wanting to gain knowledge of specific processes and roles. Each module achieves four credits:

- **Planning, protection and optimization (PPO)** Including capacity management, availability management, IT service continuity management, information security management, and demand management
- **Service offerings and agreements (SOA)** Including service portfolio management, service level management, service catalogue management, demand management, supplier management, and financial management for IT services
- **Release, control and validation (RCV)** Including change management, release and deployment management, service validation and testing, service asset and configuration management, knowledge management, request fulfilment, and change evaluation
- **Operational support and analysis (OSA)** Including event management, incident management, request fulfilment, problem management, access management, service desk, technical management, IT operations management and application management.

Candidates may take units from either of the streams to accumulate credits.

To complete the Intermediate level, the Managing Across the Lifecycle course (five credits) is required to bring together the full essence of a lifecycle approach to service management, consolidating knowledge gained across the qualification scheme.

10.4   ITIL EXPERT

Candidates automatically qualify for an ITIL Expert certificate once they have achieved the prerequisite 22 credits from Foundation (the mandatory initial unit) and Intermediate units (including Managing Across the Lifecycle, the mandatory final unit). No further examinations or courses are required.

10.5   ITIL MASTER

The ITIL Master qualification validates the capability of the candidate to apply the principles, methods and techniques of ITIL in the workplace.

To achieve the ITIL Master qualification, the candidate must be able to explain and justify how they selected and individually applied a range of knowledge, principles, methods and techniques from ITIL and supporting management techniques, to achieve desired business outcomes in one or more practical assignments.

To be eligible for the ITIL Master qualification, candidates must have reached the ITIL Expert level and worked in IT service management for at least five years in leadership, managerial or higher-management advisory levels.

11 Related guidance

This chapter summarizes the frameworks, best practices, standards, models and quality systems that complement ITIL practices.

11.1 ITIL GUIDANCE AND WEB SERVICES

ITIL is part of a portfolio of best-practice guidance published by TSO. Further information, including the ITIL glossary, can be found at:

www.axelos.com

11.2 QUALITY MANAGEMENT SYSTEM

It is helpful to align service management processes with any quality management system already present in an organization. Total Quality Management (TQM) and ISO 9000:2005 are widely used, as is the Plan-Do-Check-Act (PDCA) cycle, often referred to as the Deming Cycle.

More information can be found at www.iso.org and www.deming.org

11.3 RISK MANAGEMENT

Every organization should implement some form of risk management, appropriate to its size and needs. Risk is usually defined as 'uncertainty of outcome', and can have both positive and negative effects. *Management of Risk* (M_o_R), ISO 31000, Risk IT and ISO/IEC 27001 all provide guidance related to risk management. See Appendix G in *ITIL Service Operation* for further description of risk management.

11.4   GOVERNANCE OF IT

Governance defines the rules, policies and processes an organization needs to follow, and makes sure they are implemented consistently.

There are two ISO standards that relate to governance. ISO 9004 provides board and executive level guidance, and ISO/IEC 38500 provides for corporate governance.

11.5   COBIT

Control OBjectives for Information and related Technology (COBIT) is a governance and control framework for IT management. COBIT looks at what needs to be achieved, and ITIL provides complementary guidance about how to achieve it.

Further information can be found at www.isaca.org and www.itgi.org

11.6   ISO/IEC 20000 SERVICE MANAGEMENT SERIES

ISO/IEC 20000 is the standard for ITSM, applying to both internal and external service providers, although the standard is currently to be extended with the development of Parts 3 and 4:

- ISO/IEC 20000-1:2011 Part 1: Service management system requirements
- ISO/IEC 20000-2:2012 Part 2: Guidance on the application of service management systems
- ISO/IEC 20000-3:2012 Part 3: Guidance on scope definition and applicability of ISO/IEC 20000-1
- ISO/IEC 20000-4:2007 Part 4: Process reference model
- ISO/IEC 20000-5:2010 Part 5: Exemplar implementation plan for ISO/IEC 20000-1

- ISO/IEC 20000-10:2013 Part 10: Concepts and terminology
- BIP 0005: A manager's guide to service management
- BIP 0015: IT service management: self-assessment workbook (currently assesses against ITIL V2, to be revised via ITIL V3 complementary publications).

These documents provide a standard against which organizations can be assessed and certified with regard to the quality of their ITSM processes.

An ISO/IEC 20000 certification scheme was introduced in December 2005. A number of auditing organizations are accredited within the scheme to assess and certify organizations as compliant to the ISO/IEC 20000 standard and its content. The standard and ITIL are aligned, and ITIL best practices can help an organization looking to achieve ISO accreditation.

Further information can be found at www.iso.org or www.isoiec20000certification.com

11.7   ENVIRONMENTAL MANAGEMENT AND GREEN AND SUSTAINABLE IT

IT is a major user of energy, but can also support cultural and environmental changes as part of a green initiative. Green IT is about environmentally sustainable computing, from design through to disposal.

ISO 14001 is a series of standards related to an environment management system. Further details can be found at www.iso.org

11.8   ISO STANDARDS AND PUBLICATIONS FOR IT

There are many ISO standards and publications with relevance for IT and ITIL. Further details can be found at www.iso.org

Relevant examples include:

- ISO 9241: covers aspects that may affect the utility of a service
- ISO/IEC JTC1: deals with IT standards and publications
- The SC27 sub-committee develops ISO/IEC 27000, which relates to information security management
- The SC7 sub-committee develops other relevant standards including ISO/IEC 20000 (service management), ISO/IEC 15504 (process assessment or SPICE) and ISO/IEC 19770 (software asset management).

11.9 ITIL AND THE OSI FRAMEWORK

The Open Systems Interconnection (OSI) framework was developed by ISO at the same time as ITIL V1 was written. Common expressions such as installation, moves, additions and changes (IMAC) are OSI terminology, although IT practitioners may not realize this.

11.10 PROGRAMME AND PROJECT MANAGEMENT

Programme management can be used to deliver complex pieces of work, using interrelated projects. *Managing Successful Programmes* (MSP®) provides guidance related to programme management.

Portfolio, Programme and Project Offices (P3O®) provides guidance on managing these three areas together.

Project management guidance is found in *Managing Successful Projects with PRINCE2®* and the Project Management Body of Knowledge (PMBOK).

More information on MSP, P3O and PRINCE2 can be found at:

www.axelos.com

Further information on PMBOK can be found at:

www.pmi.org

11.11 ORGANIZATIONAL CHANGE

The organizational aspects of IT change need to be considered to ensure that changes are successful. Kotter's eight steps for organizational change (www.johnkotter.com) are referenced in *ITIL Service Transition* and *ITIL Continual Service Improvement* (Cabinet Office, 2011). See section on further guidance for details.

11.12 SKILLS FRAMEWORK FOR THE INFORMATION AGE

Skills Framework for the Information Age (SFIA) provides a common framework for IT skills. This supports job standardization, skills audits and skills planning exercises.

SFIA is a two-dimensional matrix showing areas of work and levels of responsibility. Further information can be found at www.sfia-online.org

11.13 CARNEGIE MELLON: CMMI AND ESCM FRAMEWORKS

The Capability Maturity Model Integration (CMMI) is a process improvement approach applicable to projects, divisions or entire organizations.

The eSourcing Capability Model for Service Providers (eSCM-SP) is a framework to improve the relationship between IT service providers and customers.

SCAMPI assessments can be carried out against CMMI–Standard CMMI Appraisal Method for Process Improvement. More information can be found at www.cmmiinstitute.com

11.14 BALANCED SCORECARD

The balanced scorecard approach to strategic management was developed by Drs Robert Kaplan and David Norton. It views an organization from four perspectives to balance out the financial perspective which drives many decisions. The perspectives are:

- Learning and growth
- Business process
- Customer
- Financial.

The scorecard can be applied to IT quality performance and service operation performance. More information can be found at www.scorecardsupport.com

11.15 SIX SIGMA

Six Sigma is a data-driven process improvement approach. It identifies defects that lead to improvement opportunities. Six Sigma tries to reduce process variation. It has two primary sub-methodologies:

- DMAIC – define, measure, analyse, improve, control
- DMADV – define, measure, analyse, design, verify.

Further information can be found online, including Six Sigma overviews and training.

Further guidance and contact points

TSO

PO Box 29
Norwich NR3 1GN
United Kingdom
Tel: +44(0) 870 600 5522
Fax: +44(0) 870 600 5533
Email: customer.services@tso.co.uk
www.tso.co.uk

_it_SMF UK

150 Wharfedale Road
Winnersh Triangle
Wokingham
Berkshire RG41 5RB
United Kingdom
Tel: +44(0) 118 918 6500
Fax: +44(0) 118 969 9749
Email: publications@itsmf.co.uk
www.itsmf.co.uk

BEST PRACTICE WITH ITIL

The ITIL publication portfolio consists of a unique library of titles that offer guidance on quality IT services and best practices. The ITIL 2011 lifecycle suite (five core publications) comprises:

Cabinet Office (2011). *ITIL Service Strategy*. The Stationery Office, London.

Cabinet Office (2011). *ITIL Service Design*. The Stationery Office, London.

Cabinet Office (2011). *ITIL Service Transition*. The Stationery Office, London.

Cabinet Office (2011). *ITIL Service Operation*. The Stationery Office, London.

Cabinet Office (2011). *ITIL Continual Service Improvement*. The Stationery Office, London.

ABOUT *it*SMF

*it*SMF is the only truly independent and internationally recognized forum for IT service management professionals worldwide. Since 1991 this not-for-profit organization has been a prominent player in the ongoing development and promotion of IT service management best practice, standards and qualifications. Globally, *it*SMF now boasts more than 6,000 member companies, blue-chip and public-sector alike, covering in excess of 70,000 individuals spread over more than 50 international chapters.

Each chapter is a separate legal entity and is largely autonomous. *it*SMF International provides an overall steering and support function to existing and emerging chapters. It has its own website at:

www.itsmfi.org

The UK chapter has more than 8,000 members: it offers a flourishing annual conference, online bookstore, regular regional meetings, seminars and special interest groups and numerous other benefits for members. Its website is at:

www.itsmf.co.uk

ABOUT TSO

TSO is one of the largest publishers by volume in the UK, publishing more than 9,000 titles a year in print and digital formats for a wide range of clients.

TSO has a long history in publishing best-practice guidance related to project, programme and IT service management – including ITIL and PRINCE2 – and is the official publisher for AXELOS. To accompany the core products, TSO also produces a range of complementary products to help users and organizations in their adoption of best practice. Details of all publications can be found at:

www.axelos.com

Glossary

A candidate is expected to understand the following terms after completing an SOA course.

These terms are as defined in the standard ITIL glossary. The core publication titles (*ITIL Service Strategy, ITIL Service Design, ITIL Service Operation, ITIL Service Transition* and *ITIL Continual Service Improvement)* included in parentheses at the beginning of the definition indicate where a reader can find more information.

accounting

(*ITIL Service Strategy*) The process responsible for identifying the actual costs of delivering IT services, comparing these with budgeted costs, and managing variance from the budget.

agreed service time (AST)

(*ITIL Service Design*) A synonym for service hours, commonly used in formal calculations of availability.

agreement

A document that describes a formal understanding between two or more parties. An agreement is not legally binding, unless it forms part of a contract.

availability management (AM)

(*ITIL Service Design*) The process responsible for ensuring that IT services meet the current and future availability needs of the business in a cost-effective and timely manner. Availability management defines, analyses, plans, measures and improves all aspects of the availability of IT services, and ensures that all IT infrastructures, processes, tools, roles etc. are appropriate for the agreed service level targets for availability.

billing

(*ITIL Service Strategy*) Part of the charging process. Billing is the activity responsible for producing an invoice or a bill and recovering the money from customers.

budgeting

The activity of predicting and controlling the spending of money. Budgeting consists of a periodic negotiation cycle to set future budgets (usually annual) and the day-to-day monitoring and adjusting of current budgets.

business capacity management

(*ITIL Continual Service Improvement*) (*ITIL Service Design*) In the context of ITSM, business capacity management is the sub-process of capacity management responsible for understanding future business requirements for use in the capacity plan.

business continuity management (BCM)

(*ITIL Service Design*) The business process responsible for managing risks that could seriously affect the business. Business continuity management safeguards the interests of key stakeholders, reputation, brand and value-creating activities. The process involves reducing risks to an acceptable level and planning for the recovery of business processes should a disruption to the business occur. Business continuity management sets the objectives, scope and requirements for IT service continuity management.

business impact analysis (BIA)

(*ITIL Service Strategy*) Business impact analysis is the activity in business continuity management that identifies vital business functions and their dependencies. These dependencies may include suppliers, people, other business processes, IT services etc. Business impact analysis defines the recovery requirements for IT services. These requirements include recovery time objectives, recovery point objectives and minimum service level targets for each IT service.

business objective

(*ITIL Service Strategy*) The objective of a business process, or of the business as a whole. Business objectives support the business vision, provide guidance for the IT strategy, and are often supported by IT services.

business relationship manager (BRM)

(*ITIL Service Strategy*) A role responsible for maintaining the relationship with one or more customers. This role is often combined with the service level manager role.

business unit

(*ITIL Service Strategy*) A segment of the business that has its own plans, metrics, income and costs. Each business unit owns assets and uses these to create value for customers in the form of goods and services.

capacity management

(*ITIL Continual Service Improvement*) (*ITIL Service Design*) The process responsible for ensuring that the capacity of IT services and the IT infrastructure is able to meet agreed capacity- and performance-related requirements in a cost-effective and timely manner. Capacity management considers all resources required to deliver an IT service, and is concerned with meeting both the current and future capacity and performance needs of the business. Capacity management includes three sub-processes: business capacity management, service capacity management, and component capacity management.

capital cost

(*ITIL Service Strategy*) The cost of purchasing something that will become a financial asset – for example, computer equipment and buildings. The value of the asset depreciates over multiple accounting periods.

change proposal

(*ITIL Service Strategy*) (*ITIL Service Transition*) A document that includes a high level description of a potential service introduction or significant change, along with a corresponding business case and an expected implementation schedule. Change proposals are normally created by the service portfolio management process and are passed to change management for authorization. Change management will review the potential impact on other services, on shared resources, and on the overall change schedule. Once the change proposal has been authorized, service portfolio management will charter the service.

change window

(*ITIL Service Transition*) A regular, agreed time when changes or releases may be implemented with minimal impact on services. Change windows are usually documented in service level agreements.

charging

(*ITIL Service Strategy*) Requiring payment for IT services. Charging for IT services is optional, and many organizations choose to treat their IT service provider as a cost centre. *See also* charging policy.

charging policy

(*ITIL Service Strategy*) A policy specifying the objective of the charging process and the way in which charges will be calculated.

continual service improvement (CSI)

(*ITIL Continual Service Improvement*) A stage in the lifecycle of a service. Continual service improvement ensures that services are aligned with changing business needs by identifying and implementing improvements to IT services that support business processes. The performance of the IT service provider is continually measured and improvements are made to processes, IT services and IT infrastructure in order to increase efficiency, effectiveness and cost effectiveness. Continual service improvement includes the seven-step improvement process. Although this process is associated with continual service improvement, most processes have activities that take place across multiple stages of the service lifecycle.

contract

A legally binding agreement between two or more parties.

core service

(*ITIL Service Strategy*) A service that delivers the basic outcomes desired by one or more customers. A core service provides a specific level of utility and warranty. Customers may be offered a choice of utility and warranty through one or more service options. *See also* service package.

cost centre

(*ITIL Service Strategy*) A business unit or project to which costs are assigned. A cost centre does not charge for services provided. An IT service provider can be run as a cost centre or a profit centre.

cost element

(*ITIL Service Strategy*) The middle level of category to which costs are assigned in budgeting and accounting. The highest-level category is cost type. For example, a cost type of 'people' could have cost elements of payroll, staff benefits, expenses, training, overtime etc. Cost elements can be further broken down to give cost units. For example, the cost element 'expenses' could include cost units of hotels, transport, meals etc.

cost management

(*ITIL Service Strategy*) A general term that is used to refer to budgeting and accounting, and is sometimes used as a synonym for financial management.

cost model

(*ITIL Service Strategy*) A framework used in budgeting and accounting in which all known costs can be recorded, categorized and allocated to specific customers, business units or projects. *See also* cost type; cost element; cost unit.

cost type

(*ITIL Service Strategy*) The highest level of category to which costs are assigned in budgeting and accounting – for example, hardware, software, people, accommodation, external and transfer. *See also* cost element; cost unit.

cost unit

(*ITIL Service Strategy*) The lowest level of category to which costs are assigned; cost units are usually things that can be easily counted (e.g. staff numbers, software licences) or things easily measured (e.g. CPU usage, electricity consumed). Cost units are included within cost elements. For example, a cost element of 'expenses' could include cost units of hotels, transport, meals etc. *See also* cost type.

CSI register

(*ITIL Continual Service Improvement*) A database or structured document used to record and manage improvement opportunities throughout their lifecycle.

customer agreement portfolio
(*ITIL Service Strategy*) A database or structured document used to manage service contracts or agreements between an IT service provider and its customers. Each IT service delivered to a customer should have a contract or other agreement that is listed in the customer agreement portfolio.

customer asset
Any resource or capability of a customer.

customer portfolio
(*ITIL Service Strategy*) A database or structured document used to record all customers of the IT service provider. The customer portfolio is the business relationship manager's view of the customers who receive services from the IT service provider.

customer-facing service
(*ITIL Service Design*) An IT service that is visible to the customer. These are normally services that support the customer's business processes and facilitate one or more outcomes desired by the customer. All live customer-facing services, including those available for deployment, are recorded in the service catalogue along with customer-visible information about deliverables, prices, contact points, ordering and request processes. Other information such as relationships to supporting services and other CIs will also be recorded for internal use by the IT service provider.

depreciation

(*ITIL Service Strategy*) A measure of the reduction in value of an asset over its life. This is based on wearing out, consumption or other reduction in the useful economic value.

differential charging

A technique used to support demand management by charging different amounts for the same function of an IT service under different circumstances. For example, reduced charges outside peak times, or increased charges for users who exceed a bandwidth allocation.

direct cost

(*ITIL Service Strategy*) The cost of providing an IT service which can be allocated in full to a specific customer, cost centre, project etc. For example, the cost of providing non-shared servers or software licences. *See also* indirect cost.

downtime

(*ITIL Service Design*) (*ITIL Service Operation*) The time when an IT service or other configuration item is not available during its agreed service time. The availability of an IT service is often calculated from agreed service time and downtime.

effectiveness

(*ITIL Continual Service Improvement*) A measure of whether the objectives of a process, service or activity have been achieved. An effective process or activity is one that achieves its agreed objectives.

efficiency

(*ITIL Continual Service Improvement*) A measure of whether the right amount of resource has been used to deliver a process, service or activity. An efficient process achieves its objectives with the minimum amount of time, money, people or other resources.

exception report

A document containing details of one or more key performance indicators or other important targets that have exceeded defined thresholds. Examples include service level agreement targets being missed or about to be missed, and a performance metric indicating a potential capacity problem.

external customer

A customer who works for a different business from the IT service provider. *See also* external service provider; internal customer.

external service provider

(*ITIL Service Strategy*) An IT service provider that is part of a different organization from its customer. An IT service provider may have both internal and external customers.

financial year

(*ITIL Service Strategy*) An accounting period covering 12 consecutive months. A financial year may start on any date (for example, 1 April to 31 March).

fixed cost

(*ITIL Service Strategy*) A cost that does not vary with IT service usage – for example, the cost of server hardware. *See also* variable cost.

indirect cost

(*ITIL Service Strategy*) The cost of providing an IT service which cannot be allocated in full to a specific customer – for example, the cost of providing shared servers or software licences. Also known as overhead. *See also* direct cost.

internal customer

A customer who works for the same business as the IT service provider. *See also* external customer; internal service provider.

internal rate of return (IRR)

(*ITIL Service Strategy*) A technique used to help make decisions about capital expenditure. It calculates a figure that allows two or more alternative investments to be compared. A larger internal rate of return indicates a better investment.

internal service provider

(*ITIL Service Strategy*) An IT service provider that is part of the same organization as its customer. An IT service provider may have both internal and external customers.

IT steering group (ISG)

(*ITIL Service Design*) (*ITIL Service Strategy*) A formal group that is responsible for ensuring that business and IT service provider strategies and plans are closely aligned. An IT steering group includes senior representatives from the business and the IT service provider. Also known as IT strategy group or IT steering committee.

marginal cost

(*ITIL Service Strategy*) The increase or decrease in the cost of producing one more, or one less, unit of output – for example, the cost of supporting an additional user.

net present value (NPV)

(*ITIL Service Strategy*) A technique used to help make decisions about capital expenditure. It compares cash inflows with cash outflows. Positive net present value indicates that an investment is worthwhile.

notional charging

(*ITIL Service Strategy*) An approach to charging for IT services. Charges to customers are calculated and customers are informed of the charge, but no money is actually transferred. Notional charging is sometimes introduced to ensure that customers are aware of the costs they incur, or as a stage during the introduction of real charging.

opportunity cost

(*ITIL Service Strategy*) A cost that is used in deciding between investment choices. Opportunity cost represents the revenue that would have been generated by using the resources in a different way. For example, the opportunity cost of purchasing a new server may include not carrying out a service improvement activity that the money could have been spent on. Opportunity cost analysis is used as part of a decision-making process, but opportunity cost is not treated as an actual cost in any financial statement.

outcome

The result of carrying out an activity, following a process, or delivering an IT service etc. The term is used to refer to intended results as well as to actual results.

pattern of business activity (PBA)

(*ITIL Service Strategy*) A workload profile of one or more business activities. Patterns of business activity are used to help the IT service provider understand and plan for different levels of business activity. *See also* user profile.

planned downtime

(*ITIL Service Design*) Agreed time when an IT service will not be available. Planned downtime is often used for maintenance, upgrades and testing.

priority

(*ITIL Service Operation*) (*ITIL Service Transition*) A category used to identify the relative importance of an incident, problem or change. Priority is based on impact and urgency, and is used to identify required times for actions to be taken. For example, the service level agreement may state that Priority 2 incidents must be resolved within 12 hours.

profit centre

(*ITIL Service Strategy*) A business unit that charges for services provided. A profit centre can be created with the objective of making a profit, recovering costs, or running at a loss. An IT service provider can be run as a cost centre or a profit centre.

project

A temporary organization, with people and other assets, that is required to achieve an objective or other outcome. Each project has a lifecycle that typically includes initiation, planning, execution, and closure. Projects are usually managed using a formal methodology such as PRojects IN Controlled Environments (PRINCE2) or the Project Management Body of Knowledge (PMBOK). *See also* project portfolio.

project portfolio

(*ITIL Service Design*) (*ITIL Service Strategy*) A database or structured document used to manage projects throughout their lifecycle. The project portfolio is used to coordinate projects and ensure that they meet their objectives in a cost-effective and timely manner. In larger organizations, the project portfolio is typically defined and maintained by a project management office. The project portfolio is important to service portfolio management as new services and significant changes are normally managed as projects.

real charging

(*ITIL Service Strategy*) A charging policy where actual money is transferred from the customer to the IT service provider in payment for the delivery of IT services. *See also* notional charging.

service acceptance criteria (SAC)

(*ITIL Service Transition*) A set of criteria used to ensure that an IT service meets its functionality and quality requirements and that the IT service provider is ready to operate the new IT service when it has been deployed.

service capacity management (SCM)

(*ITIL Continual Service Improvement*) (*ITIL Service Design*) The sub-process of capacity management responsible for understanding the performance and capacity of IT services. Information on the resources used by each IT service and the pattern of usage over time are collected, recorded and analysed for use in the capacity plan.

service contract

(*ITIL Service Strategy*) A contract to deliver one or more IT services. The term is also used to mean any agreement to deliver IT services, whether this is a legal contract or a service level agreement. *See also* customer agreement portfolio.

service culture

A customer-oriented culture. The major objectives of a service culture are customer satisfaction and helping customers to achieve their business objectives.

service design

(*ITIL Service Design*) A stage in the lifecycle of a service. Service design includes the design of the services, governing practices, processes and policies required to realize the service provider's strategy and to facilitate the introduction of services into supported environments. Service design includes the following processes: design coordination, service catalogue management, service level management, availability management, capacity management, IT service continuity management, information security management, and supplier management. Although these processes are associated with service design, most processes have activities that take place across multiple stages of the service lifecycle.

service design package (SDP)

(*ITIL Service Design*) Document(s) defining all aspects of an IT service and its requirements through each stage of its lifecycle. A service design package is produced for each new IT service, major change or IT service retirement.

service hours

(*ITIL Service Design*) An agreed time period when a particular IT service should be available. For example, 'Monday–Friday 08:00 to 17:00 except public holidays'. Service hours should be defined in a service level agreement.

service improvement plan (SIP)

(*ITIL Continual Service Improvement*) A formal plan to implement improvements to a process or IT service.

service knowledge management system (SKMS)

(*ITIL Service Transition*) A set of tools and databases that is used to manage knowledge, information and data. The service knowledge management system includes the configuration management system, as well as other databases and information systems. The service knowledge management system includes tools for collecting, storing, managing, updating, analysing and presenting all the knowledge, information and data that an IT service provider will need to manage the full lifecycle of IT services.

service level requirement (SLR)

(*ITIL Continual Service Improvement*) (*ITIL Service Design*) A customer requirement for an aspect of an IT service. Service level requirements are based on business objectives and used to negotiate agreed service level targets.

service level target

(*ITIL Continual Service Improvement*) (*ITIL Service Design*) A commitment that is documented in a service level agreement. Service level targets are based on service level requirements, and are needed to ensure that the IT service is able to meet business objectives. They should be SMART, and are usually based on key performance indicators.

service option

(*ITIL Service Design*) (*ITIL Service Strategy*) A choice of utility and warranty offered to customers by a core service or service package. Service options are sometimes referred to as service level packages.

service owner

(*ITIL Service Strategy*) A role responsible for managing one or more services throughout their entire lifecycle. Service owners are instrumental in the development of service strategy and are responsible for the content of the service portfolio.

service package

(*ITIL Service Strategy*) Two or more services that have been combined to offer a solution to a specific type of customer need or to underpin specific business outcomes. A service package can consist of a combination of core services, enabling services and enhancing services. A service package provides a specific level of utility and warranty. Customers may be offered a choice of utility and warranty through one or more service options.

service reporting

(*ITIL Continual Service Improvement*) Activities that produce and deliver reports of achievement and trends against service levels. The format, content and frequency of reports should be agreed with customers.

stakeholder

A person who has an interest in an organization, project, IT service etc. Stakeholders may be interested in the activities, targets, resources or deliverables. Stakeholders may include customers, partners, employees, shareholders, owners etc.

statement of requirements (SOR)

(*ITIL Service Design*) A document containing all requirements for a product purchase, or a new or changed IT service.

supplier

(*ITIL Service Design*) (*ITIL Service Strategy*) A third party responsible for supplying goods or services that are required to deliver IT services. Examples of suppliers include commodity hardware and software vendors, network and telecom providers, and outsourcing organizations. *See also* underpinning contract.

supplier and contract management information system (SCMIS)

(*ITIL Service Design*) A set of tools, data and information that is used to support supplier management.

support hours

(*ITIL Service Design*) (*ITIL Service Operation*) The times or hours when support is available to the users. Typically, these are the hours when the service desk is available. Support hours should be defined in a service level agreement, and may be different from service hours. For example, service hours may be 24 hours a day, but the support hours may be 07:00 to 19:00.

supporting service

(*ITIL Service Design*) An IT service that is not directly used by the business, but is required by the IT service provider to deliver customer-facing services (for example, a directory service or a backup service). Supporting services may also include IT services only used by the IT service provider. All live supporting services, including those available for deployment, are recorded in the service catalogue along with information about their relationships to customer-facing services and other CIs.

total cost of ownership (TCO)

(*ITIL Service Strategy*) A methodology used to help make investment decisions. It assesses the full lifecycle cost of owning a configuration item, not just the initial cost or purchase price. *See also* total cost of utilization.

total cost of utilization (TCU)

(*ITIL Service Strategy*) A methodology used to help make investment and service sourcing decisions. Total cost of utilization assesses the full lifecycle cost to the customer of using an IT service. *See also* total cost of ownership.

underpinning contract (UC)

(*ITIL Service Design*) A contract between an IT service provider and a third party. The third party provides goods or services that support delivery of an IT service to a customer. The underpinning contract defines targets and responsibilities that are required to meet agreed service level targets in one or more service level agreements.

unit cost

(*ITIL Service Strategy*) The cost to the IT service provider of providing a single component of an IT service. For example, the cost of a single desktop PC, or of a single transaction.

user profile (UP)

(*ITIL Service Strategy*) A pattern of user demand for IT services. Each user profile includes one or more patterns of business activity.

value chain

(*ITIL Service Strategy*) A sequence of processes that creates a product or service that is of value to a customer. Each step of the sequence builds on the previous steps and contributes to the overall product or service.

value network

(*ITIL Service Strategy*) A complex set of relationships between two or more groups or organizations. Value is generated through exchange of knowledge, information, goods or services. *See also* value chain.

variable cost

(*ITIL Service Strategy*) A cost that depends on how much the IT service is used, how many products are produced, the number and type of users, or something else that cannot be fixed in advance.